T0116991

Prophetic Scriptures of Jesus' Return

The Lord God is love filled with mercy and grace for all. He is the author and creator of love, charity, peace, hope, thanksgiving, and forgiveness. He is the essence of devotion to the world, as He gave His only begotten Son, Jesus Christ, as the redemptive price for our salvation. But for those who choose otherwise and willfully continue in unrighteous transgression of His commandments, and knowingly turn their back on the grace of Jesus, they fall prey to the dark demonic world and eternally fall from the eternal light of God's heavenly paradise. This book provides the many worldly and sinful violations that presently plague the world and how one can ready for Jesus' rapture, regardless of his or her past trespasses.

Those who do not believe in the rapture should read 1 Thessalonians 4:15–18 and Hebrews 9:28.

> **1 Thessalonians 4:15–18** For the Lord Jesus Himself with a word of command, with the voice of an archangel and with the trumpet of God will come down from heaven, and the dead in Christ shall rise first. Then we who are alive will be caught up together with them in the clouds to meet the Lord in the air. Thus we shall always be with the Lord. Therefore console one another with these words.

> **Hebrews 9:28** Jesus Christ was sacrificed once to take away sin, will appear a second time, not to take away sin, but to bring salvation to those who eagerly await his return.

Those who believe time has delayed Christ's returning rapture should read 2 Peter 3:3–9.

> **2 Peter 3:3–9** In the last days, scoffers will bellow, "Where is the promise of His coming?" They know not that the present earth is reserved for the final judgment and the destruction of the godless. They know not that a thousand years to a human on earth is like one day to the Lord in heaven. There is no delay in His coming.

Jesus' Rapture is Coming Soon!

The Coming Rapture of Jesus!

William Loyal Warren

Jesus' Rapture is Coming Soon!
The Coming Rapture of Jesus!

Copyright © 2010 William Loyal Warren.

iUniverse books may be ordered through booksellers or by contacting:

iUniverse
1663 Liberty Drive
Bloomington, IN 47403
www.iuniverse.com
1-800-Authors (1-800-288-4677)

Because of the dynamic nature of the Internet, any web addresses or
links contained in this book may have changed since publication and
may no longer be valid. The views expressed in this work are solely those
of the author and do not necessarily reflect the views of the publisher,
and the publisher hereby disclaims any responsibility for them.

Any people depicted in stock imagery provided by Thinkstock are
models, and such images are being used for illustrative purposes only.
Certain stock imagery © Thinkstock.

ISBN: 978-1-4502-3381-1 (sc)
ISBN: 978-1-4502-3382-8 (e)

Scripture quotations marked KJV are from the Holy Bible,
King James Version (Authorized Version). First published
in 1611. Quoted from the KJV Classic Reference Bible,
Copyright © 1983 by The Zondervan Corporation.

Scripture quotations marked NASB are taken from the *New American
Standard Bible*®, Copyright © 1960, 1962, 1963, 1968, 1971, 1972, 1973,
1975, 1977, 1995 by The Lockman Foundation. Used by permission.

Print information available on the last page.

iUniverse rev. date: 07/31/2017

Contents

Not All Is Doom and Gloom

Jesus loves you!

When reading this book, keep in mind that it is not all gloom and doom. It may be the final condemnation of those who choose not to repent of their sinful ways and accept Jesus Christ as their Lord and Savior. But for those who know and believe that Almighty God sent His only begotten son, Jesus Christ, into the world as a last and only redemptive salvation from the end-time unfolding of catastrophic judgment, this is the great—and not the terrible—day of the Lord.

It is great for those who choose to believe … and terrible for those who choose otherwise.

The Book of Revelation is the closing curtain of life as we know it. It is God's promise of pronounced judgment on all who turned their backs on the Lord God's scriptures and His only begotten son, Jesus Christ.

So, be not afraid of the coming events, for you who are under the protective wing of the Lord Jesus can continue in your peace, joy, and assurance that He will protect you.

But do try and lead others to salvation, for it will cover a multitude of your own sins. Be ready for Jesus' rapture!

Isaiah 30:18 The Lord is waiting to show you favor, and He rises to pity you. For the Lord is a God of justice. Blessed are all who wait for Him.

An Angelic Warning

This angelic warning is given to all who follow the way of the evil one.

Woe, woe, woe unto you, you demons who know of God yet mock Him with your demonic deeds on the face of the earth, for the Lord Jesus Christ comes with His sword and His angels filled with righteous wrath and indignation.

Woe, woe, woe unto you, Satan, the beast and the antichrist, of your murderous, idolatrous, deceiving ways, for the right hand of God comes, and you will be cast into the bottomless pit, the lake of fire and sulfur, and the blood of Christ will cover your throne.

And woe, woe, woe unto you, inhabitants of the earth, who turned your back on God and followed the way of the evil one, for your name will not be written in the Lamb's Book of Life, and you will be cast outside the gates of heaven, where you will wail and weep and gnash your teeth in great anguish and despair.

This is the final warning to all who oppose God and do not accept His only begotten Son as their Lord and Savior. The final curtain of life, as you know it is about to close.

You can step on the stage (wherever you are) this very moment and (1) ask the Lord God to forgive you of your past sinful thoughts, words and deeds, (2) accept Jesus as your Savior, and (3) ask for the Holy Spirit of God to enter into your soul. Or, you can expect to reap the apocalyptic eternal punishments listed.

Remember, Christ's <u>grace</u> is unmerited favor. Neither you nor I, nor anyone else, deserves it. Let not your pride or the devil hold you captive with the thought you do not deserve Christ's grace.

All you have to do is follow the above three steps and you are safely home bound for heaven.

Psalm 1:6 The Lord watches over the way of the just, but the way of the wicked vanishes.

Personal

In the beginning was the Word, and the Word was with God, and the Word was God. John 1:1-2

John was sent to bear witness of the Word and the Light of the world. Jesus created the world, but the world knew him not. John 1:1-11

Writing about the Second Coming of the Lord Jesus Christ is not an easy thing to do. I know of the various "lion's dens" that await me on the completion of the book. I know this from previous experiences in performing works for the Lord. I once built a Bible walk through a forest and spent many hours in various courts defending its existence. Many people were healed, but it did not deter those who were vehemently against the spiritual and physical aid it gave its visitors.

My sympathy is with those who do not know of the Lord and will feel the pain and horrible consequences of the end-time tribulation. People will be so afraid that their knees will knock, and their bowels will gush out in stark terror of the unchecked demonic powers.

Like many who have gone before me to prophesize the Word of the Lord, I tried to escape the prompting to do so. But slowly yet surely, one thing led to another, and it was fruitless to avoid his calling for me to spread His Word.

My youth had many extraordinary interventions and miracles that, as the years passed, made me realize something much, much bigger than I was protecting me for an eventual spiritual commission. I am physically fearful of the coming events but spiritually bold enough to continue with courageous obedience to what my preordained future holds in store. Persecution and sacrifice, along with physical and mental agony, all of which potentially prefaces eventual martyrdom as a reward to those who are spiritually commissioned by the Lord God to obey and do His will.

Judge not those who rise up against me, O Lord, for they know not what they do nor who is guiding their hideous hatred. For thy will must be done.

Deuteronomy 30:8 You, however, must again heed the Lord's voice and carry out all his commandments which I now give to you.

Foreword

A thousand years on earth is like one day unto the Lord in heaven; so 365,000 days passes for us here on earth, while only one day passes for the Lord in heaven. In essence, if the Lord told you, "I'll be back with you in one second," that one second would be equivalent to 4.22 days of human waiting.

Light travels 186,000 miles per second. The Lord is the light of the world. He can decrease that speed or increase it. Einstein said, "If one increases the speed of light, he can reverse time." If an astronaut traveled at an induced speed for a number of years, he would come back younger than his peers on earth. In conclusion, since the Lord God can increase or decrease the speed of light, He lives in the present, past, and future all at one time. Blows your mind, doesn't it?

Now take the universe of stars. There are millions of galaxies with millions of stars in each galaxy. Each galaxy is millions of light-years apart, and one light-year travels about 5.9 trillion miles. What's the point? The point is that the Lord God knows each star in the entire universe of galaxies by name, yet we have a hard time reciting the names of all our relatives.

Speaking of relatives, the Lord (your brother) also knows your name, age, weight, height and the number of hairs on your head.

Some people (even some theologians) say that, "The thousand years of man is like one day to God, and other speed-of-light factors are not to be taken literally." Well, wait until they see the omnificent, omnipresent, omniscient, omnipotent powers of Almighty God. Even then, His encompassing powers will be too much for them to totally comprehend.

This book was written in such a nature to stay away from names, dates and places as much as possible that sometimes casts too many facts and a confusing shadow over what is trying to be said. So, it basically sticks with the conclusive concept about each factor that signifies time is drawing nigh!

Yes, indeed, Jesus is coming soon, and then we will be able to see those unfathomable, sovereign powers for ourselves.

2 Peter 3:8 Do not ignore the fact that one thousand years of mankind on earth is but one day to the Lord God in heaven.

An Introductory Statement

The purpose of this book is not to judge but to merely share with the reader scripturally what and who is right in the eyes of the Lord God. I am but a mere messenger of the Lord. As you well know, He is the final judge.

Once before I was led by the Lord to warn people about something they were doing wrong. At first, I sheepishly backed off and tightly closed my lips. Then, a voice said, "If you saw a busload of people speeding toward a washed-out bridge, would you warn them?"

I quickly answered, "Yes."

"Would you be responsible if you did not?"

Again, I replied, "Yes."

Then, after a slight pause, I was told, "The people of whom I speak are heading toward a spiritually washed-out bridge, and if you do not tell them, I am going to hold you personally responsible."

Needless to say, I then boldly told the people about their wrongdoings.

It is my utmost and intense desire to warn the people who read this book that many of them are heading toward that spiritually and eternally washed-out bridge. You can put on your brakes of repentance and ask for pardon for what you have done, and the Lord will forgive you. But heed this warning: do not go back that way again! Find other, helpful, ways to spend your time. Many people do volunteer work at hospitals and other such places to replace their bad and sinful habits of the past.

And, yes indeed, Jesus is coming soon! Get yourself spiritually rapture ready.

Jeremiah 1:5 Before I formed you in the womb, I knew you. Before you were born, I dedicated and appointed you a prophet to the nations.

How Life Began ... and Its Woes

In heaven, the Lord God decided to create a human form called man. The elders and others foretold the many grievances such a creation could and would manifest. No one knows the mystery behind God's decision to go ahead and form the human being, but there was a lot of spiritual disharmony in doing so. This was especially true when the Lord God said, "I will have my angels serve the needs of man."

Almighty God's angels consisted of Archangels, Cherubim, Seraphim, Powers, Principalities, Virtues, Thrones, Dominions, and angelic beings called Angels. And He designated a guardian angel for each human being. The angels are beyond man's ability to count them as they are too numerous, and their duties and formations are beyond one's imagination.

One of the highest, brightest, and most elite angel was Lucifer. He was exulted above all other angels. And that is where the woe of troubles began. For Satan, on hearing of God's announcement that the angels were to serve man's needs, denounced the commandment, as he felt too high and mighty to serve a mere human being. Satan did not understand that serving man was not a subservient job; it was a noble assignment as man needed protection from all the hazardous elements in the world.

Almighty God already knew that the pride of Satan would rule against serving mankind, but, as mentioned previously, the Lord had the backup of all the other angels versus Satan and his fallen angels' (demons') attempts to hamper man's existence.

In a final battle in heaven, Satan and one-third of the

angels were tossed out of the kingdom of God to the earth below. And woe, woe, unto the people of the earth below, for Satan knew his time was short in proving his disobedience.

Psalm 91:9–11 Because the Lord God is my refuge, there shall be no evil befall me, for He has given His angels protection over me.

So, it is Satan and his angelic followers (demons) who thwart mankind on earth. Did not Satan, the wily serpent, trick Adam and Eve into eating the forbidden fruit and got them evicted from the Garden of Eden? And Satan, to this day, reminds God of man's ineptness in living a righteous life. He even brought despair and disease on Job for a period of 27 years to prove to God that man was not worth creating. But Job's unconquerable spirit overcame Satan's craftiness and proved to the Lord that mankind had enough unwavering and honorable integrity to justify His creation of them.

While Satan's disobedience would not serve mankind, the only begotten Son of God did obediently serve man's needs. And that person, Jesus Christ (God incarnate) not only served man, He gave His life for all of us.

So the spiritual saga continues with Satan and his demons causing all the troubles, problems, sins and unrighteousness on the earth, while Jesus with His angels work to solve and aid the Lord's people.

Shown in the following pages are the many environmental problems that plague the world as well as the unrighteous deeds presently committed on earth by many of those who do not adhere to the Word of God, or who, most regrettably, are not even of the "seed" of Father God. These sinful ways, political intrigue and environmental signs biblically depict the end times about to be brought on those who commit heinous crimes and violations of God's commandments.

If you are committing any of the following unrighteous acts, you should repent and ask God for forgiveness and get Jesus' rapture ready. For time truly is drawing nigh

Romans 10:9-10 If you shall confess with your mouth that Jesus is Lord, and believe in your mouth that Jesus is Lord, and believe in your heart that God raised Him from the dead, then you are saved. This mouth confession has brought you into salvation.

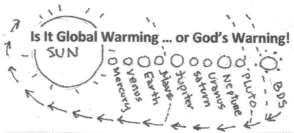

Is It Global Warming ... or God's Warning!

Almighty God always gives a warning before destruction comes forth. The Lord God told us that in the latter days the stars will fall, the earth will tremble from earthquakes, volcanos, tsunamis, tornadoes, hurricanes and people's heart will sink into despair.

Shown above is our Solar System. There are 60 thousand + such Solar Systems in our Milky Way Galaxy. And about half of those Solar Systems have two Suns.

Our Solar system is of no exception as It too, most probably, has two Suns ---our **Sun** and another Sun called the **Brown Dwarf Star, BDS.** It is called so, as the BDS does not have the fusion capability of our regular Sun. But the BDS does have seven planets orbiting it.

However, here is the destructive capability of the BDS.

As shown in the above illustration, the BDS is right outside our Solar System ... but it is still within the gradational pull of the bigger Sun.

And every 2,100 years (some astronomers say 3,600 years) The BDS orbits our Sun CLOCKWISE. The problems here is that our planets (including Earth) orbits our Sun COUNTER CLOCKWISE.

Obviously such a dichotomy in opposite orbits will cause massive polarization and total holocaust on the Earth. This may have happened to Atlantis, the Mayans and other ancient civilizations such as Sodom and Gomorrah

Whenever a civilization turns its back on the Lord God's precepts, it reaps universal repercussions. Right now there are being built underground bunkers and dome shaped housing to prepare for such an occurrence of the BDS.

If we as Almighty God's people stop backsliding into sin, the BDS will backslid back out into space. But, if not, then Father God will allow the BDS to orbit the Sun, and all who accept His only begotten Son, Jesus Christ (Yeshua) as their Lord and Savior (and repent and ask for forgiveness) will be "Rapture Up" before the BDS apocalyptically hits.

(1)
The Proliferation of Homosexuality

THE PATIENCE OF THE LORD abruptly ends when the sin of a given person, people, or country becomes full blown. Every sin is equal in its unrighteousness. But when a person decides to "legalize" his or her sin in direct opposition to the Lord's commandments, the individual is driving fool speed into a spiritual brick wall.

The gay rights movement has financially and politically organized itself into moral and legal acceptance by the courts and society. There are even special interest groups backing their push for equal marriage status. The push is on in the courts, schools, government, church and communities. It is estimated that more gays (per square mile) live in the District of Columbia than possibly in any other place in the country. By congregating near Washington DC, they can better influence any gay rights votes in Congress.

Of significant importance here is the fact that you cannot buy grace. While one can buy his way into society through bought government and media manipulation, one can never buy his or her way into heaven. The gate there is only purchased through deep reflection, repentance, the acceptance of Jesus Christ --- and living God's word.

In the 1950s, the Kinsey Report erroneously stated that 10 percent of the U.S. population was gay. Today's figures correctly show that only 2.3 percent of the U.S. population is gay. And there appear to be as many lesbians as there are gay men. But the Lord God says, "Homosexuality is an abomination and worthy of death." The Lord is not speaking of human and earthly capital punishment. No, He is talking about the "second death." The second death is when the Lord Jesus sits on the end-time throne at the right hand of Father God and decides who is not written in the Book of Life and is separated from the Lord God and written in the Book of Death. Those written in the Book of Death will be cast out of heaven where they will wail and weep in great anguish and despair.

The projected suicide rate among homosexuals is four times the rate of heterosexuals. This statistic is brought to the forefront to ward off any homosexual from taking his or her own life. The Lord God loves you. Always remember that. Your sin is no worse than that of others. Keep close to the Lord Jesus. Keep the faith. Keep praying. Never let go of Jesus. Ask Jesus to free you of your sin, and He will bring you through anything and everything. His word cannot return void.

According to the Centers for Disease Control and Prevention, gay and bisexual men and women account for one of the top majorities for contracting the AIDS virus. The AIDS virus can remain dormant for ten years and then suddenly rampage through one's infected body with deadly mutation that cannot be totally corrected at this point in time.

There is no scriptural justification for anyone to harm a gay man or lesbian or make harsh remarks about them. And it is also imperative that parents do not dismiss or cut off gay or effeminate offspring, as parental intercessory prayers provide the love and hope of God's merciful grace. However, in no way should the gay community expect society, let alone the church, to condone or be part of its scripturally unrighteous manner of living, for that would bring judgment also on those who condone their immoral acts.

Personally, one wonders if a person such as a judge, politician, attorney clergy or whoever works to promote the advance of homosexuality, for the embitterment or profitability of themselves ever consider his or her possible peril of eternal judgment.

It matters not whether something is politically correct. If the Lord God says it's wrong—then it's wrong!

There is no satisfaction in condemning or pronouncing judgment on the gay life. Unlike some judges, clergy and politicians who fan the gay lifestyle for their own financial protection or advancement, the Word of God is conveyed to help gays and lesbians realize the pending destruction of their earthly body and eternal soul.

Almighty God's does not want anyone separated from His blessings and grace. We are all sinners. We fall prey to thought, word and deed many times. But we do not try to legalize our faults. Almighty God never compromises truth, but we are to never give up trying. But many historians and theologians conclude that the proliferation of homosexuality is one of the strongest signs of the end time. *This was so forebodingly told in Mathew 24:37 As it was in the days of Noah, so it will be at the coming of the Son of Man.* Bear in mind this scripture also relates to adultery and other immoral and unrighteous acts.

Judge not the homosexuals; instead, give them ample warning of Almighty God's awaiting judgment. My heart goes out to them that they will refrain from their lifestyle. And ask them to pray to the Lord for me, as I, as well as their parents, do for them.

Leviticus 18:22 You shall not lie with mankind as with womankind as it is an abomination.

Psalm 51:1–2 Have mercy upon me, O God, according to your loving kindness, according to your multitude of tender mercies, blot out my transgressions.
Wash me thoroughly from my iniquity, and cleanse me from my sin.

(2)
Unethical Judges and Legal System

THE LEGAL SYSTEM SPILLED OVER the spiritual levy when it declared the Ten Commandments are illegal where posted on government property because of the secular misinterpretation of Thomas Jefferson's declaration of "the separate wall between church and state." In reflection, the government property belongs to the people as their hard earned taxes paid for each and every building. So the people's referendum vote should make the Ten Commandment decision, not the governing body or judicial courts.

Almighty God gave us the Ten Commandments as a moral, civil guide to keep us on the right side of life's highway. Knowing that Satan could induce all (and I mean all) people to violate the Ten Commandments, Father God sacrificed His only begotten Son for the remission and salvation of our souls.

Jesus is grace. Grace means unmerited favor. We do not deserve His grace; it is bestowed on us as a gift from Father God. But to unethical judges and the secular legal system, all this appears as a fantasy or storybook tale.

What is driving the unethical, unworthy judges is politics. Vast amounts of monies are given to various political parties in favor of minority philosophical viewpoints thus giving rise to the onslaught of incompetent, unethical judges.

Former despots, who wielded unchecked and unrighteous power in the past, took control of six basic areas: (1) the judicial system, (2) the governing body, (3) the military, (4) the banking/ monetary system and (5) the media. And they surrounded the first five areas with (6) theologically false religious and spiritual values so the people felt as if they were not running contrary to the will of God.

So you see, evil is very deceiving. It makes you feel as if what is occurring is for your safety and overall goodwill.

This brings up the story of the woman who, after she received a disappointing verdict, asked the judge after receiving a disappointing verdict, "Where is the justice?" The judge turned to her and pointing upward replied, "Justice is not here, madam. Justice is up there. The court of law is down here, and it is temporary, but justice up there remains eternal."

Judges and those who work to build the false wall between the church and state are doing so not for your safety and goodwill but for their own unrighteous, ill-conceived benefit. These are people who have eyes that do not see and ears that do not hear. Such judges make a straight line crooked with their false vision of life.

Thomas Jefferson said, "An unchecked judicial system leads to an oligarchy," which means a government run by a few people bent on self-serving philosophical and monetary benefits.

Congress has the power, given by the Constitution, to regulate and checkmate runaway, liberal judges. Judges do not make federal, state, or local laws; they merely interpret the laws laid down by Congress and signed into law by the president. But today's liberal judges are *making* the laws as well as *interpreting* them. Congress and the president must put a stop to this outrage of unchecked liberal, runaway justice.

Psalm 82:2–4 How long will you judge unjustly and favor the cause of the wicked? You should defend the afflicted and render proper justice.

Proverbs 31:9 Open your mouth. Judge righteously and plead the cause of the poor and needy.

(3)
Satanic Cult Groups

Satanic cult groups are surfacing and popping up their ugly heads of unrighteousness across America and the world. Many world religions worship false gods, but the cult groups are fiendish and diabolically evil in their obsession to serve the devil to the point, in some cases, of sacrificing human life. Countries such as Belgium, France, Germany, Greece, and Russia have laws that identify certain religions as cults or minority sects bent on destroying or altering their lifestyle. This is a dangerous practice, as that country may deem any religious group to be unsatisfactory. Unfortunately, the freedom of religion causes many to take advantage of people through false pretenses, but Almighty God remains comfortably on His throne and sovereign in that He is the one true God. (Is it a coincidence that the above countries are part of the European Union, with the exception of Russia?)

Abortion is an evil human sacrifice (immolation) in the eyes of the Lord God. Even though unscrupulous doctors and the various racket-ridden and shameless institutions have legalized it through corrupt and unprincipled legislatures and morally bankrupt and degenerate judges, abortion is a secular, human-sacrificing and immolating cult.

Anything that is demonic is nothing to play games with at any time or any place. During a motel stay, the Lord showed me what the demons looked like. I was awakened about 3:00 A.M. and inside the dim motel room were twenty or so demons walking around. They were so hideous and hateful that the room pulsated with their murderous, bloodthirsty behavior. Some were thin, and some were round like a balloon. And they appeared to be three to four feet in height and were ugly as sin. They could not rest, as they were anxious to commit some grotesque, cut-throat slaughter. I knew right then if I were to write about demonic forces, the Lord God wanted me to witness them firsthand to fully understand their murderous behavior.

A story was told in which the Reverend John Wesley (1703–1788) was sleeping one night and heard a rocker going back and forth outside his bedroom. Lighting a candle, he went to investigate. There rocking back and forth in the rocker was Satan himself. Reverend Wesley looked at hellish Lucifer and said, "Oh, it's only you," and went back to bed.

One has to admire Reverend Wesley's bravado, but I have to tell you that I had to turn on the light which immediately dissipated the spiritual evil in the room and kept that light on as I slept the remainder of the night. (It is worthy noting that historic men and women of the Lord often slept in caves by candlelight, so as not to be plagued by demons.)

This story is brought to your attention, as those who attend séances and other medium divinations have no idea of the horrific nature of demon possession stirred up during such meetings.

One should be very wary and steer clear of fortune tellers, Ouija boards, tarot cards, horoscopes, astrology, and other modes of fortune-telling. For the most part, they are demonic in nature. And in many cases, the future foretold comes true, as the demons bring about such happenings and work to covet the soul of the believer. It is spiritually wrong to incorporate any kind of soothsaying prognostications into one's life, as the Lord God wants his people to live in faith not in demonic divination (occult knowledge). For once the devil gets a person to believe in fortune-telling of any kind, his main goal is to destroy the individual and his soul. (You can search the Internet for more information about fortune-tellers, the occult, abortion, and Satanic cults).

It is this kind of satanic cult behavior that is permeating youth and adult behavior in America and abroad. On lifting those who are "born again" by the Holy Spirit of God during the tribulation, all those who chose not to believe in Christ will be unmercifully plagued by those Satanic demons day and night. And I do not want to see anyone plagued by such catastrophic horror.

If you want out of any cult repent and pray for Jesus' intercession and get up and leave. No one or thing will plague you anymore. Prayer and knowledge of God's commandments replaces temptation. No sin is beyond the forgiveness of the Lord God.

Jude 1:14 Behold the Lord comes to pass judgment on the godless.

Proverbs 3:7 Be not wise in thy own eyes; fear the Lord and depart from evil.

(4)
Worldwide Terrorism

MANY HAVE PRONOUNCED WHO THEY felt might be the Antichrist over the centuries. It ranged from Nero, Napoleon and Hitler to modern-day despots. With the advent of Muslim terrorist activity, some theologians and atomic clock authorities lean heavily on the idea that the Antichrist might surface from the Islamic Edomite section of the globe.

Herod was an Edomite as were other evil-hearted tyrannical rulers. The Edomites are an anathema to Almighty God for not allowing Moses and the Israelites to cross over their land during the Jewish Exodus from Egypt to the Promised Land. An ecclesiastic curse has been pronounced upon them as condemnation of their refusal to help the wandering Israelites during the Old Testament historical trek.

Muslim terrorists are more likely to listen to another Muslim than to any Jewish, Christian, or other religious leader when it comes to laying down arms and military proliferation. This places the land of Edom (descendants of Esau) as the place where the Antichrist might rise up and become a world leader of peace.

This thought is brought forward to would-be terrorists, "I firmly believe your Allah would prefer you save or make fifty people's lives more joyful than blasting them to smithereens. Just stop and meditate on that before you fragment another body." Sometimes just a smile or opening a door for someone can help make her day. Question is, Does your Allah want you to help his people or hurt them? Down deep. I think you know the answer. In any event, the people of Israel and other parts of the world will be so devastated and emotionally worn down by the relentless, terrorist violence that they will greet the allegedly peace-loving, deceiving Antichrist with worldwide open arms.

It is not anyone's intention to put the people of Edom in a bad light, for there are many good and bad people there and in every part of the world. I personally traveled through Egypt, Jordan, Israel, and other parts of the Middle East and found the majority of the citizens peaceful and mindful of others. They have their cultural differences, but they relentlessly work to support their family and country. It is the few in every country who Satan is able to possess and send on missions to destroy the good that exists.

All countries should prepare their people for terrorist activity that may be operating in their land. Having their people keep a sharp lookout for any terrorist activity (and having a special type phone or special e-mail reporting system) can definitely reduce or completely stop destructive jihad, a holy war in the name of Islam.

In America alone, there are Islamic terrorist compounds located throughout the country. Congress has its head buried in the sand in relation to exposing these supposedly peaceful, homegrown Islamic radicals for fear of alarming the general public. The government is afraid to expose such radically Islamic institutions—which, incidentally, are (would you believe) tax-deductible organizations—just waiting for the time to use large, extensive military weapons and explosives to detonate subway, power generating stations, bridges, and other pertinent operations as well as poisoning water systems. Wake up, America. Time is drawing nigh!

Will the Antichrist rise out of Edom? No one knows for sure, or the day, or the hour. But you can be sure that the Antichrist will appear and provide peace and supernatural miracles for three and a half years eventually declaring himself as God. He will then tyrannically rule the next three and a half years and demand that all who serve him receive the 666 mark on their hand or forehead. But those who have accepted Jesus Christ as their savior and king will not be here to witness it, for they will have been taken up into heaven at the sound of the angel's trumpets. By Jehovah, it will be a glorious time to be Jesus' rapture ready!

2 Corinthians 6:14 Do not be yoked with those who are unbelievers, for what partnership does righteousness have with lawlessness?

Proverbs 16:7 When a man's ways please the Lord, He makes even his enemies be at peace with him.

(5)
Abortion (Immolation) Clinics

MANY PEOPLE DO NOT KNOW that many abortion clinics are operated by the mafia. They finance the clinics from behind-the-scene monetary institutions.

Neither do they know that the Lord God said, "If you harm one of my little ones, it would be better if a millstone were tied around your neck and you be tossed into the ocean."

The proponents of abortion say the fetus is not a person. And our federal legal system agreed with them, as the judge said that nowhere in the Constitution does it say that a fetus is a person. The reason the justice of the U.S. Supreme Court said the fetus is not a person is because, --- if the fetus is a person, it did not receive its due process rights under the Fourteenth Amendment. Under due process, one's life (abortion) cannot be taken without a trial.

Now the Lord God said, "I know you even before you are in your mother's womb." Now if the fetus is known as a person by the Lord God before it is in the womb, how much more is it a person once it is in the womb.

The point is that the fetus does not receive its constitutional Fourteenth Amendment right of due process of law when it is aborted by an abortion clinic, with the unrighteous and erroneous legalization of our Supreme Court. But the main point is that man is now overstepping God's commandments and replacing them with his own interpretations. Woe unto that judge and those who sided with this decision, for they will surely burn in the pits of hell if they do not repent and try to reverse such a horrible law.

Ancient civilizations sacrificed their children (immolation) as offerings to false gods for favorable and financial gains. Are we not doing the same thing today? People have an abortion because it interferes with their lifestyle. They financially and socially gain something in their mind by aborting the fetus. It is immolation in the darkest sense.

If you have had an abortion or perform abortions, you can repent and ask for God's forgiveness. Some of the world's most notorious abortionists have changed their ways and found forgiveness. And women across the world who have had abortions, find peace by repenting and asking the Lord for forgiveness. But nevertheless, abortion is a sign of the end times. And it is worth remembering that abortion is not a way of life … it is, instead, a way of death.

Matthew 18:6 It would be better a millstone be tied around a person's neck and be tossed into the ocean than hurt one of my little ones.

Psalm 51:14 Deliver me from blood guiltiness, O God, my God of my salvation; and my tongue shall sing aloud of your salvation.

(6)
Rapacious Greed

GREED IS AN EXCESSIVE DESIRE to acquire or possess something in a covetous manner. It could be an overwhelming desire for wealth, power, the opposite sex, or a number of other tangible or intangible things.

Greed can be applied to a person, family, government, judicial system, or even a country. Its tentacles are stretching mainly in the business sector of America and across the globe. If you were to compare the prices of materials, gas, stocks, real estate, or any other item used in today's industry, you would see a profit spike like never before. No one wants to make a profit: they want to make a killing. They want to gouge the marketplace.

At one time, business people were paid and promoted when they could come up with ideas and concepts that saved the buyers money and gave them more comfort and convenience. Nowadays, the bean counters sit and continuously trump up ways to make the consumer pay more and get less for their purchased service or product. I tell you this: the company that serves the consumer first will win profit wise in the short and long run.

The itch in the palm of today's industry is a gluttonous one. Penny-pinching executives who figure out ways to skin the consumer will eventually run amuck. Executives who can create innovative ways to make the consumers better off financially, and their own net worth will immediately rise.

It is well worth remembering that the Lord God does not use great ideas and talents that are contrary to the good of His people. No, He looks for the companies and executives who find and innovate ways so His people do not perish. If greed is permeating itself in your organization, have a meeting and discuss ways to help your marketplace and, simultaneously, yourself. And if your executives cannot come up with those ways, you have the wrong group of people working for you.

Greed is one of the seven deadly sins. But, please keep in mind that an individual's industry and hard work to accomplish a given financial goal does not constitute greed. It is when done at the disadvantage of others and for unchecked, glutinous profit that the sin of greed enters the scene. Yes, greed is another sign of the end times.

Proverbs 10:9 He who walks honestly walks securely, but he whose ways are crooked will fare badly.

Psalm 18:23–24 I was upright before Him, and I kept myself from my iniquity. Therefore, the Lord recompensed me according to my righteousness.

(7)
Adulterous Affairs and Fornication

PEOPLE DO NOT BELIEVE THAT evil spirits can enter their body upon having an affair with another person. It matters not if the person is single, married, homosexual, or bisexual. Believe it—it's true. Whether you are married or not, fornication, or adultery, is a sin, whereby you open your body to house a potential host of evil spirits.

When Jesus stopped the stoning of Mary Magdalene, He cast out the evil spirits that possessed her. And He told her not to return to her old sexual ways lest she become possessed by even more demonic spirits. And since Jesus told that to Mary Magdalene, it applies to all of us equally as well.

Jesus spoke even further about lust and adultery when he said, "Thou shall not commit adultery, but I say unto you, even if you look on a person lustfully, you already committed adultery in your heart."

Adultery is so bad that it is the only reason the Lord Jesus said a person can divorce his or her spouse. He knew the demonic activity it can generate in a family and its offspring.

Now there is forgiveness.

If a person chooses to forgive his or her adulterous spouse, and that adulterer repents and becomes righteously true in marriage, the sin is forgiven by the Lord God. But, the adulterer should find a pastor to exorcize any demonic spirit that may have entered him or her during the affair. Forgiveness is one of the highest forms of Godliness. It must be done without any harboring of resentment. Yes, it can be done, for all things are possible for those who trust in the Lord.

Adulterous affairs come about when one falls prey to greed, pride, and lust. When you were a kid, you may have wanted someone's marbles. As you get older, the greed for someone else's spouse is not much different than the want of the marbles as a kid. Then, the sin of lust takes over the person along with pride in that he (like the devil) feels he can personally violate God, who said, "Let no person put asunder that which I put together."

Forgiveness can be received from the Lord God by repentance of the sin of adultery, and from one's spouse --- if true sorrow and marital fidelity are assured.

The building blocks of any marriage, partnership, or contract are based on faith, hope, and love. These building blocks will never stand the ill winds of life if they are not cemented with forgiveness and forgetting. Otherwise, the building blocks of any togetherness will crumble at the first seemingly unpardonable mistake or unforgivable blunder.

I was listening to a sermon from a pastor in Orlando, Florida. He held up a $20 bill. Then he asked who wanted it. Everyone raised their hand. The pastor then placed the $20 bill on the floor and jumped up and down on it. On picking it up, he spit on the $20 bill and rubbed it in some dirt. Again, he asked, "Now who wants this $20 bill?" Once more, almost all the hands went up in the air. Then the pastor said, "You accept this $20 bill filled with grime and dirt, but you will not take back someone who offended you, who is priceless in worth to the Lord." Again, the pastor paused and asked, " Is there anyone who has ever offended you that you should forgive and take back more than this dirty $20 bill?"

It is worth remembering you will need a *ton* of forgiveness when you step forward and come face to face with the Lord Jesus at the End-Time Throne. Does not the Lord's prayer say, "Forgive me of my trespasses, as I forgive those who trespassed against me?"

He will know all your past thoughts, words and deeds when you humbly stand before Him.

And He will see how well you handled any "pierced hearts" you may have received during your journey through life. A pierced heart is when you give your very best to someone, and they disappoint or defame you. Mary, the mother of Jesus, is the mother of pierced hearts. For she gave her people her son, Christ Jesus, and they rejected her and the Lord. Mary forgave them, and you, too, must learn to forgive. When you stand before the Lord, all your pierced hearts (whereby you forgave those who grieved you) will appear as spiritual medals on your chest and thus be rewarded.

James 1:14 A person is drawn away, tempted and enticed by his or her own lust.

1 John 1:7 But, if you walk in the light of Christ and fellowship with the righteous, the blood of Christ will cleanse you of all your sins.

(8)
Vile and Unrighteous Entertainment

WATCH THE COMEDIANS ON TODAY'S TV stations. Their mouths are filled with filth and sexual overtones. And the audience applauds and cheers their immoral, verbal obscenities.

Satan uses humor in many instances to bring an unrighteous landslide of filth down upon the unsuspecting audience. Even TV sitcoms contain an overload of careless dialogue, personal acts of degeneration and reprobate behavior.

The actors and actresses seem to think that if they can get away with some verbal obscenity or act that impresses their peers, they have arrived at some kind of professional nirvana. In reality, they have corrupted the Lord's people with demonic, lewd, repugnant, and disgraceful words and behavior. And the fact that the attending audiences loudly clap and acclaim the comedian's obscene language is evidence of a society gone awry in righteous behavior.

Now, the Lord God loves humor. Humor is the twisting of a given situation, whereby it's presented by someone who has the knack of conveying the matter in a comical way—either by his or her voice inflections and physical movements of body (eyes, face, legs, or hands and arms) along with perfect timing.

All this can be done without the use of foul language. We all have been around people who use expletives in their everyday conversations. They do this from past family behaviors or maybe to impress the listener with their tough nature. But it is a cheap way to express oneself.

So it is with comedians. It seems like many of today's comedians feel they have to pepper stories with foul language to be funny and acceptable. They have little realization that, in doing so, they have allowed an evil, demonic spirit to enter their body. And that evil spirit has no rest. It will eventually bring in other spirits—such as, drugs, fornication, filth, and sloth—and more obscene aspects into their life..

The Lord's condemning finger points not only at the obscene comedian but also at the bursts of laughter from the audience who enjoys such humorous vulgarity.

The most successful stand-up comics have learned the Lord's way of telling a story without the lewd language. Comedians who have learned how to twist a given situation into the comical, without foul, obscene language and behavior, are on their way to stardom. And do not use the Lord's name in vain, for the day will not end before one is punished for doing so. In refraining from lewdness, comedian, as well as his or her audience, will begin to become rapture ready!

Ephesians 4:29 Let no corrupt communications proceed out of your mouth, but that which is good and ministers grace unto the hearers.

Psalm 34:13 Keep the tongue from evil, and the lips from speaking guile.

(9)
A Lawless Society

WITH SO MANY HOMELESS AND wayward children walking the streets without any guidance, time will soon have them violently rampaging in the streets and government buildings.

Around half the marriages in the United States end in a divorce court. In many instances, the care of the divorced couple's children is left in the hands of state institutions. And the children who are cared for by one parent or another sometimes do not receive the tender loving care that can only come from a loving, married couple.

This does not mean that all divorced parents do not love their children or that the children are not taken care of properly. Some children are better off when parents are separated, as the children do not suffer the continual arguing, abuse, and sometimes, physical fights.

But what all this does mean is that unsupervised children are roaming the country here and abroad with no moral or legal upbringing. This all adds up to a kindling environment, eventually to ignite into lawlessness and violence. When there is no love, no caring, and no one to lean on, the light at the end of life's tunnel is very dim. This depression can very easily turn into violent anger to relieve the frustration one feels inside.

Our leniency in allowing quick marriages and even quicker divorces has seeded the country into a crab grass of problems. Society must find a way to deal with the many homeless children before it is too late.

Across the world, there are approximately one hundred fifty million homeless children, walking the streets and scavenging dumps for food. They are often taken advantage of by wretched and despicable people. These lost children may be led to lawlessness and a multitude of problems, such as, rebellion, terrorism, violence, rioting, disobedience, mob rule, gangs, and other revolutionary transgressions. Right now, there are youthful gangs spreading their tentacles across the United States and globally to bring in drugs to support their violent groups.

You can break away from such a group simply by asking Jesus to enter your life and to protect you and those you love. He will put a protective spiritual web around you, and you will become rapture ready! Salvation is a step-by-step spiritual walk. And God will guide you.

If you feel lonely from the loss of parental guidance, always remember that now, and eternally, Jesus is your brother, Blessed Mary is the mother of all who come to her beloved Son, and Almighty God is your true Father. Now, who could ask for a better family? And it is yours for all eternity. Know it, believe it, receive it, and you will know the peace, joy, and love of the Lord God in your life.

1 John 3:4 Whosoever commits sin commits lawlessness, for sin is lawlessness.

Acts 5:29 You should obey the word of God rather than that of unrighteous men.

(10)
Massive Unchecked Immigration

THE BORDERS OF ALMOST ALL countries are virtually broken down when it comes to stopping illegal immigrants. Presently, Mexican migrant workers in the United States comprise 10 percent of Mexico's entire population. Last year, these migrant workers sent $20 billion their families in Mexico. That is the amount of money the United States pays annually for its entire foreign aid.

Visit parts of the country where the home building and other areas of work are abundantly available, and you will find it is overloaded with immigrant workers. Bear in mind that these immigrant workers are as industrious and effective as ants in a busy anthill. They are all over the foundations and roofs of the communities being built.

What are they going to do when a depression or deep recession hits the country? Even now, some illegal immigrants want the country to change the language to better service their communication needs. I am not condoning or condemning this request, but it does show the embryonic stage of what is to come if and when an economic storm slows or stops the economy.

France recently experienced rioting by unemployed immigrant workers. Burning and looting are not uncommon when large numbers of immigrants have no income to support their families.

Politicians play the game of seeing who can gather in immigrant votes, when they should be deciding how to end this potential tyranny.

Immigration is a great, innovative way to create new and useful ways for people to live. It provides a country with objective reasoning, which culminates in an overall better way of life. But when immigration becomes unchecked and uncontrolled, you can be rest assured that the eventual outcome will be a reign of violent protest and revolt.

Right now, this very day, border patrol officers are being sentenced to prison when they fire a weapon at immigrants, even if the border patrol's life is at stake or the illegal immigrants are smuggling in massive loads of drugs. This insanity of law must be rectified immediately.

Everyone deserves a chance to improve one's lifestyle, but it must be done according to the law. Otherwise this leads to a lawless, runaway society that is unsafe for everyone, including the diseases brought in by unchecked immigration.

American has prospered from the objective reasoning and thinking of immigrants since its inception as a country. Immigrants are an important addition to America's culture and future growth. But, like everything else, it must be done lawfully.

My prayers are for all immigrants to, some how and some way, fit in properly, profitably, and lawfully throughout the world. With prayer, this can be done.

Luke 13:24 Strive to enter in the strait gate.

Psalm 37:3 Trust in the Lord and do good; so shall you then dwell in the land, and verily you shall be fed.

$\left(11\right)$
Wars and Rumors of Wars

THERE HAVE BEEN WARS SINCE the dawn of mankind. Some military and philosophers say that wars sometimes help a society by pushing it into modern civilization. And, many contractors state that the bombing of buildings is an expedient and inexpensive way to tear down the old edifices and build up the new. While these rationales for condoning war may have a bit of truth, it is still a sad commentary on how civilization survives.

But nowadays, we are in a different era of war. Never before has there been such an expansion of violent nuclear capabilities around the world. Various countries have the nuclear capability to commit another Hiroshima against whomever and whenever they want. Countries are one thing, but it is also the individual terrorist who uncaringly strives to get hold of such nuclear devices.

Weapons of mass destruction (WMDs) in the hands of

a few terrorists can result in worldwide chaos and nuclear destruction. It is reported that the five major wars—World War I, World War II, the Korean War, Vietnam, and the Gulf War—had a death toll of over fifty-nine million. And if you add to that all the skirmishes and mad dictators around the world, that death toll number could easily double.

So, wars and rumors of wars, which have been with us for centuries, are now stark realities of massive destruction in everyone's daily lifestyle.

Years ago, a group of politicians, thought leaders, military officers, clergy, and other important people discussed the possibility of living economically and peacefully without war. The sad conclusion was—no! War seems to be a part of life. That is, until the Savior Jesus Christ brings world peace.

The Middle East has been a nuclear powder keg since it began reaping tremendous profits from exported oil. Their leaders have purchased modern planes and WMDs with newly found monies to defend themselves from onlookers jealous of their wealth and property. But, they have done little if anything to help the economic struggle of the people in their countries. To condone their ambitious greed, they seek and point out problem situations in other countries and exaggerate them in riotous speeches to their countrymen, all designed to mask their own avarice and rapacious desire for power.

Eventually, there will be jihad that will end their terrorism in what the past Israelite prophets prophesied as Armageddon—the Apocalypse! This is when the heavens open and the angels with the Lord Jesus Christ, whose eyes are like a flaming fire, ride on a white horse. Out of the Lord's mouth comes a terrible swift sword to smite the nations and bind Satan into the bottomless pit. Yes, time is drawing nigh! Get rapture ready!

Revelation 12:7–12 And there was war in heaven and Michael and his angels fought against the dragon and his angels. And the old dragon along with the Devil and Satan was cast upon the earth. Therefore rejoice in heavens, but woe to the inhabitants of the earth and of the sea, for the devil has come down unto you having great wrath as he knows his time is short.

Psalm 46:1 God is our refuge and strength; a very present help in trouble.

(12)
Earthquakes, Volcanoes, Hurricanes, and Tsunamis

THERE WERE TEN MAJOR EARTHQUAKES between 1920 and 1990, a seventy-year span. But, there were seventeen major earthquakes between 1990 and 2005, just a fifteen-year span. In fact, you may have seen the one in Hawaii on TV. Between 1960 and 2007, there were 72,106 earthquakes and 159 volcanoes; each day, 5 earthquakes of a magnitude 5 shake the earth.

A major earthquake in the Indian Ocean in 2004 caused a tsunami, in which approximately one hundred thirty thousand people lost their lives. Once again, this shows the environmental upheaval taking place around the world. One only has to look at the daily paper, which generally features a section showing the various places around the globe that were hit by a volcano, earthquake, hurricane, or other environmental tragedies.

Was the flooding of New Orleans an end-time shot across the bow of mother earth? Are there other areas in America and across the planet that sit waiting for the next violent act of nature? Of course, there always have been such catastrophes, but are they becoming more pronounced?

The answer is, unequivocally, yes!

The 2004 tsunami in the Indian Ocean had hundred-foot

high waves. During the time of Noah, some of the waves were five hundred feet high. And such magnitudes of waves may someday hit every major shoreline in the world. If earthquakes were to erupt in various places on the earth, they would literally wipe out one-third of mankind in a blink of an eye. Tsunamis stemming from such volcanic blasts would sweep hundreds of miles inland, drowning all with towering waves.

In the next twenty-five to thirty years, there will be more devastating tectonic plate shifts worldwide, causing huge tsunamis, gigantic earthquakes, and the violent eruption of volcanoes. All this, again, has been prophesied in the book of Revelation, when the second trumpet in chapter 8, verses 8 and 9, is blown by the angels.

This is the reason the tribulation is the great and terrible time of the Lord. Great for those who know Christ and accept Him as their Savior, but terrible for those who reject God's only begotten Son, Christ Jesus; their denial of Him will reap the horrible punishments of the end time.

If you tell some elitist, erudite person that it is God's angels who control the four corners of the earth, she will wittingly smile and smugly say something like, "What Mother Goose book have you been reading?"

But it *is* true. God's angels hold the environment together until that end-time moment! Know it, believe it, and be rapture ready!

Revelation 7:1 Then I saw the four angels standing at the four corners of the earth holding back the four winds of the earth.

Psalm 46:1–3 Though the earth be removed; though the waters roar, and the mountains shake with swelling, we will not fear for the Lord is our refuge.

(13)
Unprincipled Lawyers (Radical Minority Groups)

REMEMBER WHEN YOU WERE A kid and watched the old cowboy movies? The villains were caught, sent to jail, and that was the end of the movie.

Nowadays, the movie begins with the villains being caught and then unscrupulous lawyers use every legal maneuver to get them out of jail and back on their horses.

Unscrupulous lawyers, unprincipled judges, and the right to sue the police force for every imaginable reason add up to a runaway legal system. This is a perfect time for someone to overtake the legal system and utilize it for his own means.

Radical minority groups in the country, that I know by name, that you know, that they know themselves, and most important, that the Lord God knows, are, in essence, wolves in sheep's clothing. Radical minority organizations have their own lawyers bent on changing the way people think, speak, and live in America. They have instituted the "politically correct" mode of conveying the way people should speak. And it is all designed to box in the Christian way of life.

The American Center for Law and Justice (ACLJ) and the American Civil Liberties Union (ACLU) take different views on moral, political, and environmental issues. Sometimes they judicially shake hands in agreement on certain issues. It is up to you to see what side of the judicial-spiritual fence you want to be found at the end time.

In no way am I personally condemning any one organization, for the Lord has a way of implementing changes, whereby, He will, at times, use the bad to correct the good. What I am telling radical minority groups is that there is no way on this earth or in this universe that they can overrule the word and will of Almighty God. For what can anyone do to Almighty God or any of His children that won't be burned up like dry stubble?

It is beyond logic and moral reasoning that the court system is insisting that the Boy Scouts of America cannot profess their faith to Almighty God, and homosexuals are permitted to lead these young children. Woe, what fatal prophetic fate awaits the judges who enact such legal restrictions?

The fact that many of these secular humanistic organizations are inhibiting the Lord's people testifies that time is drawing nigh. The Lord told us that during the end times, there will be a people not of His seed who will follow the evil one and make changes in society contrary to His precepts.

My job is to inform you of all this insanity; for, if you vote to approve such humanistic, secular wickedness, you are an accomplice to their evil ways and are held equally responsible in the eyes of the Lord.

Be not fooled by such radical secular organizations. Instead, be rapture ready!

2 Timothy 3:8–9 Just as Jannes and Jambres opposed Moses, so also they oppose the truth … but their foolishness will eventually be plain to all.

James 3:16 For where envying and strife is, there is confusion and every evil work.

(14)
Drug/Alcohol Addiction

SOME YOUNG PEOPLE, AS WELL as some adults, think the only way to have a party and have fun is to indulge excessively in alcohol. Later, they graduate and mix various kinds of drugs with their alcoholic beverages to further induce that good feeling.

The danger of mixing alcohol and various drugs is that the user might (1) die from a respiratory shutdown, (2) experience a synergistic effect in which one drug mixed with one drink can pump up a person's metabolism as if they had ten or more drinks, (3) become dependent on a very expensive, addictive habit, (4) criminally pursue monies to continue their addiction and become dangerous to others and (5) just basically out of emotional control.

Not all addictive substances are difficult to obtain. For those who inhale substances, items such as, aerosol cleaners, gasoline, cleaning fluids, butane, and acetone are easily available. These items are listed so parents pay attention to whether they seem to be disappearing more quickly than usual, or if they are found in the house but not used for their intended purpose.

The main items of drug addiction are tobacco, alcohol, cocaine, speed, hallucinogens, inhalants, marijuana, and PCP (angel dust). Users of the mainline drugs are very dangerous to themselves and to others, as their thinking and ability to act properly are impaired. It is especially dangerous while driving under the influence of addicted drugs as it can be the cause of many fatal accidents.

In sports, I was fortunate enough to play high school, college and a little professional basketball. It was always very difficult to guard a player on drugs, for a drug (1) raises a ball player's level of expectation while it (2) lowers his inhibition. Think about that.

Such a player's elevated expectation makes him feel as if he can jump over your head and his lowered inhibition suppresses and blocks out any refrain from his doing so. However, here's the problem a drug infested player runs into.

What you use or feel on the court (or in any athletic endeavor) is what you will eventually use or feel off the court. In essence, such a player most generally runs into legal and other problems as he is basically out of control. You see, the drug raises his expectation and lowers his inhibition when he is off the court also. And that is how and where he runs head first into a legal brick wall. Many times you will read about his problem with the law in the papers.

Point being, do not use drugs. Use your faith in the talent the Good Lord gave you, and you will win both ways --- on and off the court.

The continued increase in drug trafficking and drug abuse affects the very way society survives. There will be more and more senseless killings to fulfill one's addictive needs. The cost to the country in terms of hospital and institutional help can cripple any economy.

Drugs and alcohol fill or lead to loneliness and low self-esteem as well as depression. This void can be filled with the love and spirit-filled joy of the Lord God. Hopefully, this prayer will help those who suffer from alcohol and drug addiction:

Lord, I come to you in total trust that you will deliver me from this addiction of alcohol and drugs. In you, I put my trust and faith. Thank you, Lord, for hearing my prayer and setting me free. Amen.

Romans 4:7–8 Blessed are they whose iniquities are healed and forgiven and whose sins the Lord does not record.

(15)
Pornography

PORNOGRAPHY HAS DEVASTATING EFFECTS ON the youth and adults in the country, especially on the twelve to seventeen-year-old kids. About forty million Americans watch pornography, which often makes them eventually act out the scene. And the audience is mostly comprised of men—about 72 percent in fact.

And it is only going to get worse.

The creators of pornography have now begun to perfect electronic devices, whereby the viewers can actually feel as though they are participating in sexual acts with the people on the screen.

The eventual violent outcome to society is frightening, as more and more viewers will physically and immorally begin to prey on others, doing what they see and acting out what they viewed on the screen. Immoral and molestation acts first originate in the mind, find their way in everyday discourse, and then physically manifest themselves by preying on others.

As you can see, first come the thoughts, then the words fall from the tongue, and finally, physical and sexual harm to others.

Seeing pornography on the computer or other video apparatus is the easiest way for such acts to take hold in one's mind. From there, a Pandora's Box of demonic activity opens itself in the mind of the viewer, leading him into every imaginable kind of satanic sexual activity.

To many, the only way to be free from such sexual slavery is to receive exorcism from a spirit-filled clergy. In the name of Jesus Christ, the pastor will denounce the demons that may reside within the person and cast out all that is spiritually evil within him or her.

Psalm 40:13 O Lord, deliver me and make haste to help me out of my deep despair.

In the name and power of Jesus Christ's Holy Spirit, I denounce and cast out of you that demonic spirit of pornography, fornication, homosexuality, pedophilia, adultery, drugs, alcohol, lying, cheating, stealing, and all unrighteousness behavior in thought, word, and deed. So be it. It is done. Praise ,Jesus, praise the Spirit of Wisdom, praise the Holy Spirit, and praise Father God who will send His angels to guard and comfort you.

Galatians 5:7–9 This enticement that hinders you does not come from God. For a little yeast leavens the whole batch of dough.

(16)
A Shameful, Unrighteous School System

IT IS THE YOUNG AND the innocent who the unrighteous want to swing over to their perverted way of thinking and living. Secular humanistic groups work to negate school prayer legally. There is a scripture that says, "Forever learning but never gaining the knowledge thereof." In essence, education without the Lord God is in vain at best.

In addition to negating school prayer, secular and atheistic groups want to institute homosexuality in the school system as a normal lifestyle. Indeed, they failed to read the Bible, where the Lord God says, "Homosexuality is an abomination worthy of death." The Lord is not talking about capital punishment; He is referring to the second death, whereby those who lead an evil, unrighteous life on earth are eternally separated from Father God, written into the book of death, and tossed into the eternal, fiery pit.

People do not want to see our children duped into accepting or condoning a sexually abnormal lifestyle that sends them into spiritual decay. Nor do they want to see anyone who has a sexual dysfunction deceived by the devil into not having his or her name written into the Lamb's Book of Life.

Secular and atheistic people misrepresent and spuriously utilize the "separation of church and state" clause in the Constitution as a manner and means of having their godless philosophy acceptable in the school system. This allows them to spout off their unsanctified and atheistic viewpoints, while simultaneously and legally disallowing any reference in thought, word, or deed to Almighty God's Word.

If you are a judge, lawyer, politician, PTA member, teacher, principal, parent, or anyone else and condone the homosexual lifestyle as well as embrace abortion for teenagers, you are headed for the pit of fire and sulfur—right with those who are working to legalize it.

If you strike a match and smell the sulfur content from just that tiny fire, multiply it by thousands, and you will feel, smell, and understand the immense eternal pain that hell has to offer those who defy the Lord God's Word.

The Lord knows it is your intentions to lure the youth to your unrighteous lifestyle through education and media facilities. Woe unto you who do this and to those of you who unwittingly obey such wicked, abominable practices on unsuspecting youths.

Read Leviticus 18:22, Romans 1:18–32, and Revelation 20:10–15 if you do not believe me, for there, the Word of God confirms the truth.

Yea, what can anyone do to Father God Yahweh or any of His children that it won't burn up like dry stubble.

Matthew 18:6, Luke 17:2 It is better that a millstone was hanged about his neck and he is cast into the sea and drowned than offend one of these little ones.

Psalm 25:4–5 Teach me your path, O Lord; show me your ways, and lead me to the truth.

(17)
Jerusalem Surrounded

MANY TIMES IN THE PAST, Jerusalem has been surrounded. It was surrounded by the Canaanites, the Philistines, the Assyrians, the Babylonians, the Persians, the Greeks, the Romans, the Islamic nations, as well as others. In each of those times of war, the Lord God defeated or raised the opposing armies of His people.

There will be an end-time battle over the land of Israel. The Muslim nations are looking for their jihad leader, the ruler who will allegedly lead them into victory over the people of Israel. Have they not read or studied the history of the defeated armies who tried to take the Holy Land of the Lord God? Only defeat and bewildered mortification await the Muslim world (and those nations who join them) if they again try to attack Israel.

The secretive attacks and suicide bombings of various terrorist groups will eventually cause the Muslim world to try and annihilate the Israelites with one complete frontal attack. This gigantic, frontal attack will temporarily defeat the Israelites and spread worldwide terror. The Muslims will then unwittingly feel as if they have conquered not only the Israelites but the entire world of alleged infidels.

To avoid worldwide nuclear chaos, the world leaders will accept the new Muslim leader, and a period of three and one-half years of peace will abound. But eventually, the Muslim leader (known as the Antichrist) will try to sit on the holy throne in the temple and declare himself God. He will stamp 666, the mark of the beast, on all who live and demand that they can only eat or drink if they bear that infamous mark.

After the first illustrious three and one-half years, the next three and one-half years will be filled with such fear that people's bowels will gush out, and their knees will knock from the demonic activity surrounding the Antichrist's dictatorship. For, at this time in history, the Holy Spirit of God, who protects the people from demonic activity, will be taken up along with the Lord's flock of sheep, thereby leaving the demons to torturously plague those remaining on earth.

And here is the secret, my friends: the only power and authority Satan and his demons have on earth has been given to him by the Lord God. Satan and his fallen angels' time on this earth has been calculated by Almighty God more precisely than any earthly atomic clock. The past six thousand years of mankind have been but six days to the Lord in heaven. And He is ready to stir up the world to see who will follow Him and who will follow the devil.

This is the reason the first frontal attack on Israel is a false victory for the Muslims and the nations who unite with them, because they are filled with hatred and envy of the Israelites and for the greedy takeover of the Israel's seaports and eventual oil discovery. Little do they know that the Lord has hooked them there to set up this final Armageddon, where He annihilates the nations that attack Israel.

Most theologians theorize that the spirit of God will take up His born-again Judeo Christians before the Antichrist reigns, especially before the second three and one-half-year period. Those nonbelievers remaining on earth will believe a pandemic flu or some other factor has finally rid them of the Judeo Christians.

Little do they know that the Lord raised His born-again people into heaven, and the catastrophic apocalypse of those left behind is about to begin. O Lord, thy ways are a befuddlement to mankind, but not to those who strive to live your word.

Genesis 14:20 Blessed by God Most High who delivers your foes into your hand.

Proverbs 1:33 Who harkens unto the Lord shall dwell safely, and be quiet from the fear of evil.

(18)
Many Who Are Not of the "Seed"

MORE AND MORE, YOU SEE and hear people who are not of the "seed" of Almighty God. Such people are likened to the Sadducees in the Old Testament, who did not believe in a life after death. While the Pharisees believed in an eternal spiritual life, the Sadducees did not. They are called the sad *Sad*ducees.

People who are not of the seed are easy to identify. They have eyes that do not see spiritual signs and ears that do not hear the word of God. And their heart is of stone.

They espouse their humanistic, secular philosophy on national TV and other media without any regard for the Word of God.

And they have infiltrated the court system so that their viewpoints are made arrantly and brazenly legal, while those who remain committed to scripture are unmitigated and falsely found guilty of inappropriate or politically incorrect thinking.

They advocate homosexuality as a wholesome, normal way of life, as well as the sanctioning of couples living together without the need of marital ceremony. They have little regard for the unborn and jeer those who regard the sanctity of the fetus. They shout for the separation of church and state only to ratify their secular, humanistic agenda. And they have no objection to pornography, prostitution, drug use, pedophilic behavior, drunkenness, foul language, or other abuses of civility.

Such people have also infiltrated the entertainment business, and you can easily identify them by their vile language and gross and lewd physical scenes on the screen. And they use the Lord's name in vain, with little regard or knowledge that the day does not end before a fit punishment is delivered to those who do so.

Remember and remember it well. No one, I mean no one, mocks Almighty God's words. And if they do and live, it is only because an even greater and eternal retribution awaits them, unless they repent and change their ways.

This is brought to your attention so that you do not fall into the belief that mocking the scriptures is acceptable to Father God.

The day will soon arrive when they will dearly pay for their unrighteousness here on earth as well as in eternal fire and damnation. Know you not that the unrighteous shall not inherit the kingdom of God?

All this is, again brought up so that maybe someone, somewhere out there will say to himself, "He is talking about me. And I am going to make a change with the help of Jesus Christ."

Believe me, it is never too late to ask the Good Lord to intervene spiritually on your behalf. He is always there for you. Just ask Him and get yourself Jesus' rapture ready!

Ephesians 5:5 Be sure of this, that no immoral or impure or greedy person or idolater has any inheritance in the Kingdom of Christ and of Almighty God.

Psalm 50:10 Create in me a clean heart, O Lord, and renew a right spirit in me.

(19)
Disease, Pestilence, and Plagues

SOMEWHERE IN THE WORLD, THERE is a pandemic of bird flu already out of its embryonic stage, waiting to mutate itself into a human-to-human infestation. Only acute monitoring can contain such a virulent, epidemic-type flu from quickly traveling across the globe, for nowadays jet transportation can infect millions in a matter of hours, days, or weeks.

In the twentieth century alone, twenty million people worldwide died of the Spanish flu of 1918 and the Asian flu of 1957. In addition, the Hong Kong flu of 1969 killed an estimated seventy thousand Americans, alone.

Today's "miracle drugs" (antibiotics) and vaccines promised to wipe out tuberculosis, pneumonia, malaria, smallpox and various venereal diseases, but the new strains of the same diseases now seem to be drug resistant.

And widespread, non-preventive cases of HIV are rampantly spreading across the globe. Presently, over 60 percent of the reported cases of HIV are in Africa. HIV can have an incubation period of fifteen years, and since it is constantly mutating, there is little chance of developing an effective vaccine against it.

Bird flu can kill up to 50 percent of those infected and spread from continent to continent within a matter of hours, thanks to modern transportation methods. If the bird flu mutates and becomes communicable between humans, it can kill one hundred million people within a twenty-one-day period.

The Ebola virus has an 80 percent mortality rate.

Today's "miracle drugs" (antibiotics) and vaccines promised to wipe out tuberculosis, pneumonia, malaria, smallpox, and various venereal diseases, but the new strains of the same diseases now seem to be drug resistant.

If the H1N1 avian flu mutates and becomes communicable between humans, this flu can kill 100 million people within a 21 day period.

Jesus prophesied in Luke 21:11, "And great earthquakes shall be in different places and 'pestilences' and fearful sights and signs shall appear from heaven."

There is no doubt that one should prepare for unknown, natural disease outbreaks or man-made ones by having a "survival kit" handy along with adequate food supply.

Yes, the rapid proliferation of drug-resistant diseases is a strong indicator that time is drawing nigh. Historically, plagues have always been prevalent in society, but with all the other infectious catastrophes taking place, a more acute end-time awareness of such diseases is plausible. Of great concern to today's scientists are the viruses yet to be uncovered, as the natives in the jungles cut deeper into the forest for food and farming needs.

There is no doubt that one should prepare for unknown natural or manmade disease outbreaks by having a "survival kit" handy, along with adequate food supply. But the best preventive preparedness for any kind of pestilence is to know the Lord God, Jesus Christ, and to stay tucked under His protective wings. Yea, what can anyone or anything do to Father God's children that it won't burn up like dry stubble? Yes, God protects and loves you that much!

Yes, it spiritually and medically pays to know Jesus and be rapture ready!

Deuteronomy 12:26–28 I set before you a blessing for obeying the commandments of God … and a curse if you do not obey the commandments of the Lord.

Psalm 103:3 It is the Lord who forgives all your iniquities, and who heals your diseases.

(20)
Famine and Overpopulation

RIGHT NOW, ONE-THIRD OF THE world's population of 6.7 billion people are well fed; another one-third are underfed ... and the remaining one-third are starving to the point that approximately ten million people die each year because of hunger or some related disease.

It is estimated that many of the starvation-related deaths since 1900 were caused by inept administration, theft, greed, poor storage facilities, or callous, non-caring manipulation by dictating egomaniacs.

In 2002, the United Nations gathered twenty-two economically sound nations to contribute $194 billion a year to starving nations. This would require that each of the twenty-two give 0.7 percent of their national income. Broken down, each country gives less than a penny from every $100 of national income. This amount of money could stop world hunger.

One only has to look at the bloated bellies of the children of Somalia or Ethiopia that are paraded across the screens of your TV sets to know and understand the danger that may await the entire world.

"How so?" you might ask. One answer could be global warming. Another answer could be other climate changes that can destroy many of the world's productive crop producers. World leaders have already declared that the world cannot continue to supply adequate food for its ever-increasing population.

When asked if they ever experienced a miracle, most people merely shake their heads and reply, "No. Never saw or experienced one."

It would do them well to become acutely aware that "every day" is a miracle. And when they wake up and see the sun shining through the curtains, they should say, "Yes, now I know, see and live a miracle."

It is a miracle that food is available for us from the ground and oceans, for it only takes a few degrees' temperature change (global warming) to destroy crop and sea production so that the entire world suffers from inadequate food. Some weather analysts attribute the recent snow and rain along the Atlantic coast and New England states to the continuing effect of the "El Nino" phenomenon, an unusual warming of the Pacific Ocean off the coast of South America. Is the "Greenhouse effect" caused by the emission of excessive carbon dioxide, oxygen nitrate, and methane from automobiles and industry that is prompting the changing weather?

In 1970, the U.S. Intelligence Agency predicted that due to the world's exploding population—China has 1.2 billion people; India has 1.3 billion people; Japan has 125 million people, packed 856 people per square mile, compared with Russia's 150 million people with only 18 people per square mile—along with adverse weather, a world dictator could grab power through revolution by promising adequate food for everyone.

The prophet Joel (Joel 1:17–20) spoke of a time of drought, when the cattle will die and the river will dry up. I ask you, is that time drawing nigh?

Matthew 4:4 Man does not live by bread alone, but by the word that proceeds out of the mouth of God.

Psalm 92:12–14 The righteous shall flourish like the palm tree … they shall bring forth fruit and flourish.

(21)
Explosion of Knowledge

FIRST AND FOREMOST, THE GREAT outpouring of knowledge in the last fifty years is not by mere chance. The supremacy of all this exponential knowledge is by the omnipotent, omniscient hand of Almighty God. He has a divine purpose for our good and the fulfillment of His glory.

Keep in mind that the Lord God does not look for great ideas and great talents in choosing leaders and innovators of newly found knowledge. He uses people who have a great likeness to his only begotten Son, Jesus Christ. Yes, the Spirit of God constantly searches the face of the earth to find people who are worthy to lead and create new ideas so His people do not perish.

In comparison to previous times, when knowledge doubled every ten years, it now doubles every twenty-two months. And all things, including knowledge, have one purpose: to assure that God's people will not perish and that His glory is personified.

In October 1957, the first small satellite was sent into orbit, followed not long afterward by the first manned space vehicle to orbit space. The question is, what does God have in mind in outer space exploration? Is it to show mankind the unfathomable depth of the universe equates to His incalculable, immeasurable mind?

The same is true with the radio and TV. If man can see and listen to others across the globe, cannot the Lord God see us individually and also know our thoughts, words, and deeds? And can He also see what is not only in our mind but what is hidden deep in our heart?

Through the explosion in knowledge you see in the movies, sports, music, or any aspect of life (if you look closely enough), you can somewhat decipher whether that enlightenment is purposefully given unto His people to show them what is good or what is bad for them.

Truly, though, the explosion of knowledge in the latter day is one more sign of the Good Lord's return. This is deemed true, as the proliferation of such knowledge will eventually be given into the wrong hands of satanic powers. Satan can only rule when he gets hold of computers and scientific information needed to control the human race.

The Messiah is coming soon. Get rapture ready.

1 Corinthians 3:19–20 For the wisdom of this world is foolishness in the eyes of the Lord, for it is written—He catches the wise in their own ruses, for the Lord knows that the thoughts of the wise are in vain.

Proverbs 3:13–14 Happy is the man who finds Wisdom; and who gets understanding, for she is more precious than rubies and then that of fine gold.

(22)
One New World Order

THE PROPHET DANIEL (DANIEL 2:31–45) explained the dream that greatly puzzled and disturbed the Babylonian king Nebuchadnezzar. Daniel told King Nebuchadnezzar that his dream was of a great statue. The statue's head was of gold, representing the glorious King Nebuchadnezzar of Babylon; the breast and arms of the statue were of silver, representing the Persians, who would defeat the Babylonians; the belly and its thighs were of bronze, representing the next ruler, that of the Greeks; the legs of the statue were of iron, representing the Romans; and the feet were of iron and clay, representing the combined nations at the end time.

Then a stone cut out without hands smote the statue, crushing and breaking it into pieces. The stone (Jesus Christ) will return during the final battle and completely crush the feet of iron and clay (combined nations).

The conglomerate of countries comprising the European Economic Community (the ECC, founded by Jean Monnet on January 1, 1959, and which is now part of the European Union) is headquartered in Brussels, Belgium. Today, some of the 27 countries associated with the EEC include, Greece, France, Germany, Great Britain, Ireland, Denmark, Belgium, the Netherlands, Luxembourg, Spain, Italy, and Portugal.

The book of Revelation speaks of the beast with seven heads and ten horns. A smaller beast with two horns (pretending to be like the lamb) made the people worship the first beast. The two-horned beast (the Antichrist) made the people put the mark 666 on their forehead or right hand in order to receive food.

In the books of Ezekiel (chapters 38 and 39) and Revelation (chapter 16), it is prophesied that the Russians (Gog) will come out of the north to fight against the people of Israel, along with China and Middle East countries (the feet of iron and clay), including countries comprising the EEC at that time (all the combined nations as prophesied). This army of over two hundred million soldiers will culminate at the Battle of Armageddon in Israel. According to the Bible, blood will run up the horses' bridles.

By 2010, it is estimated that the EEC, with its 345 million people, will become number one in the world economy; number two is the United States (300 million people), followed by number three, China (with 1.2 billion people). The fourth world power will be Japan (with 125 million people, with a density of 856 people per square mile).

What will bring the combined forces of various countries to attack Israel? The answer is: the Lord God will hook them there like a fish. He prophesied the end-time battle, and His Word cannot return void.

Zechariah 13:8 In all the land, says the Lord, two thirds of them shall be cut off and perish.

Proverbs 4:15 Enter not the path of the wicked or evil men; avoid it, pass not by it, turn from it and pass away.

(23)
Spiraling, Out-of-Control Medical Costs

IT IS TIME FOR PHARMACIES, insurance companies, doctors, and hospitals to change their healing approach for their patients. In today's medical world, there are ways not being offered to treat the cause, not just the effect, of many illnesses.

By not treating the cause, the medical bills are piling up beyond many people's ability to pay them.

By just treating the effect, it keeps the patient returning again and again to the doctors, who prescribe prescriptions from the pharmacy. Many times, the patient ends up in the hospital, and then must pay even more for his or her insurance.

As one can easily see, the real problem is simply not treating the cause of any given patient's illness. Overall, the doctors in the country do try in earnest to treat the cause of a patient's illness. But there are doctors who knowingly just treat the effect, as they either do not know how to treat the cause or they are purposely embezzling the patient as well as the insurance companies.

Add to this the fact that hospitals are now a business as well as a hospital. They have to keep the rooms filled as much as any hotel. Doctors associated with those hospitals are also sometimes exposed to keeping the beds filled. This is not good.

There are cases where the results of a patient examination

are exaggerated to the point that the patient is sent to the hospital for a potentially needless operation by highly paid hospital staff doctors. While this may seem hard to believe, it has happened and can happen again. This happens as the hospital hires highly paid physicians, and they must keep money coming in order to meet their salaries as well as the costs of other hospital facilities.

Hospitals, for the most part, do operate on a very professional level.

Note: Patients who misuse the advice of doctors, prescriptions, and medical facilities are also a big part of the medical cost problem.

The question is, "who is to fault here?"

Is it the doctor? Is it the pharmaceutical companies? Is it the hospitals? Is it the insurance companies? Or, is it the liability cases piling up doctor fees and insurance?

The answer lies in proper investigative regulation by the government. The government is designed to regulate, not own businesses or enterprises. Anything that is not regulated properly will run away with a slew of indiscretions, including unchecked financial improprieties.

Pharmaceutical companies must begin to develop drugs that can cure the cause, not just the effect of illnesses. By doing so, doctors will have the right medicine to treat the cause of patient illnesses.

If, however, the pharmaceutical companies fail to create medicines that cure the causes of illness, the doctors will continue just to treat the effects of patient illness, and the unchecked spiraling costs will continue to escalate out of control.

With the high costs of creating new, effective drugs (as well as the time needed to test them), pharmaceutical companies run into a bit of a catch-22. But if they were to create drugs that treat the cause instead of just the effect, the costs would come down, and their profits would remain stable, as well.

Doctors and hospitals could then better facilitate patient needs. The high costs paid to the insurance companies would also come down, and doctors would have more time to treat patients effectively.

Realistically, there is no one simple answer to the costs of doctors, hospitals, and insurance and pharmaceutical companies. But, again, one of the main answers is in treating the cause—not just the effect—of patients' illnesses. And this can be done!

It is significant to note that Jesus always treated the cause when healing people.

Mark 5:24–34 Many people crowded around Jesus. A woman who had a blood issue in her body and suffered from many physicians and spent all she had and was no better reached out and touched Jesus' garment. And straightway she was instantly healed. And Jesus said, "Who touched my garment?" The woman fell face down and trembling said, "I did." And Jesus said, "Daughter, your faith has healed you. Go in peace."

It is significant here to note that Jesus' always treated the cause when healing people.

(24)
Foreign Nations against Israel

As shown in number 17 of why "time is drawing nigh," the Muslin nations will join forces with the big two nations, that is, Russia and China. China now has a two hundred million–member army itself.

In fact, Russia and China have joined Iran at this very moment to develop nuclear reactors for Iran. Right now, Russia is building seven nuclear reactors, at a price of $10 billion for Iran. Russian and China (who, in the past, were bitter enemies) are now holding military exercises together, which include the use of submarines and strategic bombers.

Other nations (which could include the United Nations), including other Asian nations, will eventually band together to overtake Israel.

The question is why?

One answer is that they will be deceived by evil spiritual forces beyond their knowledge, as the devil hates the Israelites whom the Lord God loves.

Another answer is that the invading armies and nations will want and desire the seaport (Mediterranean Sea) to transport oil and other strategic supplies for their army and economy.

When this invading army of various nations unites against Israel, they will be comprised of two hundred million men, military machinery, and airborne equipment.

However, the Lord God will bring down fire and brimstone and totally annihilate this invading army, whereby the beast and the false prophet are tossed into the pit of fire and sulfur.

After this, a temporary treaty is put together by the United Nations, allowing the Israelites to rebuild the temple. Then, the Antichrist (who is separate from the beast and false prophet) will eventually rise up again to sit on the throne of the new temple, calling himself God.

The Antichrist will demand that all must have the mark 666 on their forehead or hand in order to eat or live. From here, he organizes another army against Israel, which again is defeated by Almighty God.

The Antichrist (devil) is then thrown into the pit of fire and brimstone with the beast and false prophet, who are already there. And a New Jerusalem is brought down from Heaven. The Lord Jesus, who will sit at the right hand of Father God, will then judge the living and the dead. Yes indeed, Jesus is coming soon!

Ezekiel 7:5–6 Thus say the Lord, disaster upon disaster! See it coming. An end is coming. An end is coming upon you. See it coming.

Proverbs 11:11 By the blessings of the upright a city is exalted; but it is overthrown by the mouth of the wicked.

(25)
Spread of God's Word Worldwide

GOD'S WORD IS SPREADING FASTER than ever before because of evangelists, missionaries, TV, radio, cell phones, autos, boats, satellites, and other electronic forms of communication. Once the entire world is reached with the very Word of God (Jesus Christ), the final end-time curtain will come down.

Spreading the gospel of Jesus Christ has always been a precarious job. The apostle Paul was whipped, deserted, imprisoned, attacked by deadly reptiles and wild animals, and suffered all the emotional and hunger pains one can imagine—besides being killed.

To be a missionary takes an unusual person who receives a calling from God and is filled with the boldness of His Holy Spirit.

Of the world's population, 33 percent are Christians, 19.6 percent are Muslims, 13.4 percent are Hindus, 12.7 percent are nonreligious, 6.4 percent are Chinese, Buddhists, 2.5 percent are atheists, 1.7 percent are new religions, 0.2 percent are Jewish, and the remaining 4.6 percent are others.

Within many non-Christian countries are small groups of Christians, who live on the edge of acceptance, impoverishment, and persecution to the point of death.

The apostle Paul said one must pray with confidence that the Lord God will open the door when and where a missionary is placed to spread the gospel of Jesus Christ. And slowly but surely, the dark that surrounds that particular place will be replaced with the "light" of the Lord.

What separates Jesus from other religious leaders—such as, Buddha, Mohammed, or Confucius—is that Jesus claimed to be the actual Son of God. Did He not say, "If you have seen me, you have seen the Father?" In John 8:19, Jesus said, "'If you knew Me you would know my Father also.'" And unlike other religious leaders, Jesus gave up His life under cruel hardship for what He believed. And eleven of His apostles also suffered an agonizing death; John died a natural death.

In the midst of His life on earth, Jesus pronounced in John 8:42, "If God were your Father, you would love me; for I proceeded for and came from God, neither came of myself, but He sent me."

It is when all Christians from all the above-listed religions and countries are reached with the gospel of Jesus Christ that the Almighty God will draw the end-time curtain.

Jesus represents grace. Grace is defined as "unmerited favor." You cannot buy grace. It is a gift from Almighty God to those who accept Jesus as their king and savior.

With the massive communications and transportation means, and the history of missionaries working throughout the world, you can very well see that time is drawing nigh.

Isaiah 9:1 The people who have waked in darkness have seen a great light. Upon those who dwell in the land of gloom, a light has shone.

Proverbs 27:20 Hell and destruction are never full; so the eyes of man are never satisfied.

(26)
Increase of World Travel, Hotels, and Restaurants

YOU CAN GO BY PLANE, you can go by boat, you can go by truck or auto, or you can go by bus ... and leave the driving to us.

Travel around the world has accelerated exponentially. Diplomats, vacationers, business executives, immigrants; you name it, and you will find that nowhere in the annals of history have people traveled so frequently.

Just in the United States alone, about 25 percent of the people doing commerce here fly in and out of the airports daily. And not only can you fly here, or practically anywhere in the world, there also are hotels and restaurants to accommodate you.

The expediency of world travel began in 1927, when Charles A. Lindbergh flew solo across the Atlantic Ocean in thirty-three and one-half hours. He did this using only a magnetic compass, in spite of the weather conditions, such as violent storms, that plague the Atlantic and a featureless body of water.

Nowadays, commercial transatlantic flights are commonplace, carrying hundreds of passengers who eat and sleep, and have restroom facilities. They can complete this Atlantic Ocean flight in four hours. And once a passenger's flight is complete, there are many hotel chains and eating places in the United States and around the world to facilitate his or her traveling experience.

Yes, it goes to show you that Almighty God generally uses one person (in any field of endeavor) when innovating or moving toward a new direction.

Not only the travel, but think also of the many chains of hotels and eating places that are set up here in the United States and around the world which also biblically indicates --- time is drawing nigh!

Aerodynamically, we have progressed to the first U.S. moon landing by the Apollo 11 craft, followed by man's first step foot on the moon on July 20, 1969.

The United States is planning a lunar base by the year 2024. We are not only expediently progressing faster and faster with world transportation, we are now in outer space with the first-ever lunar "hotel," complete with eating facilities.

So, we are now beyond the mere earthly increase in travel. We are now into outer space and traveling at a much, much greater speed.

Satan will need computerized, as well as transportation, speed to control and maintain his domination on earth. And that is one of the main reasons increased transportation is one of the signs of the end times.

The question is --- knowing that increased travel is a vital sign of the end time, do you think time is drawing nigh? In no uncertain terms, you have to sense it.

Proverbs 8:12 I, wisdom, dwell with prudence and find out knowledge to witty inventions.

Psalm 78:24–25 God rained down manna for them to eat, and man ate angels' food.

(27)
Genetic Engineering

HUMAN GENETIC ENGINEERING HAS LED scientists to uncover that thirty-five thousand genes are in each human DNA molecule, comprising 3 billion chemical bases arranged in precise order.

What mankind intends to create with this newly found DNA knowledge is what brings him closer to understanding the Lord God, or driving him further away from Him.

Psalm 100:3 says, "Know the Lord Himself is God. It is He who has made us and not we ourselves."

In order to preserve humanitarian principles, human genetic engineering reached Capitol Hill on July 31, 2001. There, the representatives of Congress enacted the Human Cloning Prohibition Act of 2001, making it unlawful to (1) perform or attempt to perform human cloning, (2) participate in attempting to perform human cloning, and (3) ship or receive products of human cloning for any purpose. Anyone violating the three laws can get up to ten years in prison and a $1,000,000 fine.

Opponents of human genetic engineering state that it is the willful killing of human embryos and, most important, leads man to usurp God's creation of man. It is important to remember that not all genetic engineering comes from the human embryo, and not all genetic engineering is devoted toward human cloning. Tremendous benefits to mankind can come from genetic engineering --- with proper procedures (from the umbilical cord) as one example.

One scientist conveyed that in no way should the scientific world allow a divine foot to step in the doorway of enlightened knowledge.

There is story where an overly religious student was hitchhiking one day and was picked up by a truck driver. The driver was smoking a cigar, and the zealous student said, "You know, if the Lord wanted you to smoke, he would have put a smoke stack on your head." At that remark, the truck driver replied, "And if he wanted you to ride, He would have put roller skates on your feet." And he promptly stopped the truck and ordered the student to get out and walk. *My point is that, in all instances, there is a proper time and place to intervene with God's Word.*

However, God does not interfere in science; He opens the door and provides creative breakthroughs. It is man who thinks he comes up with the answers, when it was really at the precise time God's divine intervention gave him the answer.

However, it is up to man to decide whether to use genetic engineering for the benefit of mankind or its destruction. For if man clones a child, does the child have a spirit? Does the child have a soul? Is man the creator of the child? Again, is man usurping God's domain? Does man have the compassionate thoughts of God for that which he creates?

And who knows what Satan will do with genetic engineering once he reigns temporarily on earth.

Psalm 139:13–17 It was you, O Lord, who created my inmost self, and put me together in my mother's womb. For all these mysteries, I thank you, for the wonders of myself and the wonders of your work. You know me through and through, from having my bones take shape when I was being formed in secret from the lowest parts of the earth. You have scrutinized my every action, and all were recorded in your book. My days are listed and numbered; even before they first occurred. How precious are your thoughts of me, O God.

(28)
The Red Heifer
(Young Unblemished Cow)

THE RETURN OF THE MESSIAH, according to Jewish law, follows the rebuilding of the temple in Israel. The first Temple was torn down by Nebuchadnezzar in the year 587 BC The second temple was destroyed by the Romans in AD 70.

Today, the third temple (for which the blueprints have been completed), the priestly garments, musical instruments, and other objects are ready. The believers of Yesha, which means the preparation to rebuild the temple, the readiness of the priestly robes, the making of the musical instruments, and other holy objects verify that the return of the Messiah is very near.

And, attempts to lay the cornerstone of the temple have been precisely predicted.

Right now, plans are being made as to the exact location of the temple so it falls in line with the first two temples. Some of the Jewish people believe that the temple will come down from heaven by itself in a flame of fire. While other Jewish scholars go by the Torah and state that the temple must be built when the time is right.

According to chapter 19 of Numbers, the fourth book of the Torah, before rebuilding the temple, all the Jewish builders must be first purified by the ashes of a red heifer, a young, unblemished cow). It is worth noting here that there had not been a red heifer born in Israel for two thousand years. However, in the year 2002, the first-ever red heifer was born in Israel as described in Numbers 19.

The believers of Yesha, which indicates the preparation to rebuild the temple, the readiness of the priestly robes, the making of the musical instruments, and other holy objects verify that the return of the Messiah is very near.

The fact that the first red heifer in over two thousand years has now been born in Israel in preparation of ashes to purify the builders of the third temple further verifies that time is drawing nigh!

One question remains. The shed blood of Jesus eternally takes the place of past sacrifices of bulls and goats. However, the use of the ashes of the red heifer to cleanse the builders and the temple is in preparation of _____. You fill in that blank. For the Antichrist will try and sit on the throne of the third temple and declare himself God.

And when the Messiah Jesus returns, he brings down a new Jerusalem.

2 Corinthians 6:16 For you are the temple of the living God; for the Lord God says, "I will dwell in you and walk in you, and I will be your God."

Isaiah 66:1 The Lord says, "Heaven is my throne, and the earth is my footstool."

Numbers 19:1–4 Bring a red heifer, without spot, wherein is no blemish. The priest Eleazar, shall slay it and sprinkle its blood directly on the tabernacle.

(29)
Worldwide Return of the Jews to Israel

IN ISAIAH 43:5–6, THE PROPHET Isaiah said the people of Israel would return to their homeland from the east, from the west, from the north and from the south.

From the east: Since Israel's independence as a country was achieved in 1948, thousands of Jews have returned to their homeland from the surrounding eastern Arab countries.

From the west: During the 1900s, hundreds of thousands of Jews fled from the west, including Western Europe, the United States, and especially from the Holocaust in Germany.

From the north: Hundreds of thousands of Jews living in the Soviet Union moved to Israel from Russia after great pressure by other nations (as prophesied by Isaiah).

From the south: A massive migration of Jews came to Israel from Ethiopia only after Israel Ethiopian Fund paid a ransom to Ethiopia (as prophesied by Isaiah).

The massive migration of the Jews throughout the world occurred when they fell away from the Lord God's precepts and were destroyed, along with their temple, by the Babylonians in 587 BC. Later, in 70 AD, the Romans sacked Israel and the temple further, sending the Jews to other countries throughout the world.

But, as the prophet Jeremiah said in Jeremiah 8:7–8, "I will save my people from the countries of the world. I will bring them back to live in Jerusalem. They will be my people, and I will be faithful and righteous to them as their God."

And today we see with our own eyes the restoration of Israel and the massive return of the Jews to their homeland after being dispersed throughout the world for nearly two thousand, nine hundred years.

It is wise to know that the people of Israel should not be judged in error, as did Balaam in the Old Testament. The error of Balaam is that he saw only the natural immorality of the Israelites and their seemingly sinfulness and concluded that the Lord God would curse them. However, the Lord God told Balaam to bless the Israelites, not to curse them, for He alone is the justifier of His chosen people. The punishment of Almighty God on the people of Israel is in itself sufficient. We cannot punish another family's children, and so it is with God's children. He alone blesses and curses the people of Israel in relation to their living or not living His Word.

Under the umbrella of Jesus' grace, we gentiles are also now brothers and sisters of God's only begotten Son and are also God's children. But, we must always remember that we were grafted onto the Jewish olive tree, whereas the Jews, who did not leave God under the Old Testament, will have their eyes opened to know Christ as the Messiah when the complete number of gentiles is grafted. In doing so, all will be subject to God's mercy and grace (undeserved merit), for who can then say to Father God Yahweh, "I made it on my own." Only the Lord God remains, and will always remain, sovereign.

You will not know the hour, day, week, month, or year of the Lord's return, but you will see the signs beforehand. Are you seeing them?

Ezekiel 34:28 And they shall no more be a prey to the heathen, neither shall the beast of the land devour them; but they shall dwell safely and none shall make them afraid.

Psalm 61:3 For you, Lord, are a shelter and a strong tower from my enemie

(30)
Corrupt, Uncaring Politicians.

THERE ARE MANY POLITICIANS WHO really care about the people they represent. However, there are also many who are mainly interested in getting reelected in any way possible.

Every time there is an election (and especially for president), you can expect to experience economic chaos via an upsurge in gasoline and oil prices. as well as massive unemployment or some other trumped-up recession or inflationary spiral.

The candidates, and those behind them, who expediently impact the economy for their own gain will certainly be accountable to the Lord God at the end time, for they caused such tremendous financial and emotional problems for the Lord's people. I sometimes wonder if they have any idea of the fires of hell that could await them for the turmoil they manifested and their underhanded dealings to get elected or reelected.

Politicians have caused people to lose their homes, jobs, savings, self-esteem, spouses, families, and even their lives. Woe unto those politicians (and those with them) who have created such economic chaos and have dealt this calamity on the people.

If a politician knows of a crooked politician who does not get caught, you can be sure the deceitful politician has lost his or her integrity, and what is gained by him here on earth will be the potential loss of their soul for all eternity. Yes, there are times when *The Devil and Daniel Webster* is not just a story by Stephen Vincent Benét. It is real!

People of the Lord get caught very fast when they try the same politically dishonest techniques, which is indicative of their being children of the Father God. He chastises them immediately.

So, envy not those politicians who use dastardly, conniving ways to accomplish anything, for their gain is only here on earth. Their loss may very well be eternal damnation.

Political correctness is nothing more than political posturing for one's own gain. Common sense tells one when certain words are not socially acceptable. To establish politically correct manners of speaking is nothing more than the eventual setting up of a way in which Satan can ultimately control the tongues of the people.

Luke 13:27–28 And the Lord shall say unto them, "I know you not. Depart from me you workers of iniquity." And they shall wail and weep and gnash their teeth as they are thrust out of heaven.

Matthew 3:2 Repent all of you, for the kingdom of heaven is at hand.

(31)
Church Leader Apostasy

O LORD, OUR DARK SECRET SINS ARE A LIGHT BEFORE YOU.
Psalms 90:8

HAVE MERCY ON ME, O LORD. BLOT OUT MY TRANSGRESSIONS.
Psalms 51:1

THE GATES OF HELL WILL never abolish the church, but inside the church are few, but nevertheless, enough men and women of the cloth who violate the very precepts of Almighty God.

Every day there are certain pastors, priests, rabbis, deacons, and others of the cloth who lie, steal, commit adultery, fornicate, engage in homosexual acts, and who commit pedophilia and other unrighteous and sinful acts.

Do they think the Lord does not see them? Do they care? Are they so demonically possessed that they have given themselves over completely to satanic behavior?

It is imperative that a person of the cloth painstakingly guards his or her thoughts, for thoughts become words, and words become deeds. And it is the thoughts that Satan infiltrates with demonic activity. The imagination can run away with one whose eyes are not trained to see only that which is spiritually sacred. Otherwise, the lust of the flesh can easily overtake one.

Demonic activity always surrounds and works diligently to overtake people around sacred places. Be it in the church, a shrine, or any holy place, you can be sure that demons are always present seeking those they can influence to desecrate that holy sanctuary.

Judge not your church, but do test those in authority to make sure they are well within the commandments of the Lord God.

The men and women of the cloth are to be revered, not worshipped. They are to be regarded with respect and honor, for they stand and intervene for you to the Lord Jesus. Woe unto anyone who disrespects any clergy member, and double and triple woe unto any clergy who falls prey to unrighteous deeds.

Fall on your face and repent, you men and women of the cloth, and confess your sin to your superior, for your thorn in the side is no less or worse than that of Saint Paul. Nothing is beyond the forgiveness of the Lord if you repent and do not go back to your original sins. It is well worth remembering this quote from Martin Luther, "While you may not be able to stop a bird of unrighteous thought from flying over your head, it does not mean that you allow it to build a nest in your hair."

1 Peter 4:18 If the righteous scarcely be saved, where shall the ungodly and the sinners appear.

2 Corinthians 7:10 Godly sorrow works repentance to salvation.

(32)
Divorced, Broken Homes

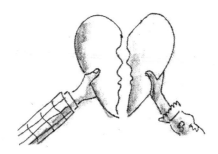

MARRIAGES SUFFER AND END WHEN one member continuously fails to use discretion in everyday dealings. The lack of foresight, along with imprudent words and actions by one's spouse, is not unlike pulling out the roots of a flower to see how well it is growing.

The Bible states, "Indiscretion in a beautiful wife or handsome husband is like having a gold ring in a pig's snoot." They always seem to return to the mud of life.

A family can be wrecked by a multitude of indiscretions, such as, alcohol, drugs, infidelity, physical or verbal abuse, lack of concern, little or no affectionate love, financial hardship, unrelenting religious or political differences, homosexuality, theft, lying, or a multitude of uncontrollable impulses.

The stress from a manic-like marital situation can lead

to depression, suicide, strokes, diseases, drug abuse, and the disruptive roots of later sibling behavior problems. In fact, children of divorced parents are more likely to have behavior problems, and are more likely to suffer from abuse, and have a greater chance of living in poverty.

No one wants to be alone, but cold feelings in a family relationship paralyze love, whereas warm feelings cuddle and nurture a marriage.

You must realize that Satan seeks to destroy the joy and peace in any and every family. His most successful tactic is to somehow—be it via an indiscriminate word or deed— humiliate, debase, disappoint, or demoralize the other spouse. Satan sets the stage for the perfect moment to charge the atmosphere and then "bang," he smacks the unsuspecting spouse with some word or act that sends him or her whirling out of emotional control.

Proverbs 23:7 As a man or woman thinks within themselves, so they are.

If such a provoked incident occurs time and again in your marriage, it is a red flag that marital counseling is needed. Self-esteem is needed in marriage as much as breathing oxygen, and it is imperative to see a born-again preacher or counselor who is spiritually in touch with the Lord Jesus Christ.

It is Jesus Christ who is your Lord, King, High Priest, Brother, Savior, Intercessor, Protector, Divine Physician, and Counselor. And His Holy Spirit and Spirit of Wisdom work through spirit-filled counselors. It is only when you and your spouse definitely and absolutely decide to follow and obey Almighty God's precepts and commandments that Satan will stop dead in his tracks and stop plaguing your marriage and family. So says the Lord, "Yea, what can anyone or thing do to my children that it will not burn up like dry stubble."

Common sense in marriage or any institution is nothing more than staying on the right side of the road regarding God's words. If you veer off the right side of the road, you can expect to have a head-on emotional collision with Satan.

Forgiveness is next to Godliness. Some say there are three basic types of love. There is the *brotherly love,* where you show affections for your parents, brothers, sisters, and relatives. Then there is the *sensual love,* where you feel physically amorous toward you spouse (but not to others). And the deepest, most spiritual love is the *agape love,* which conquers all in its forgiveness, understanding, mercy, and grace. Without agape love, it is very unlikely a marriage will last. Think of the good in your spouse, and in Jesus' name, spiritually work out the bad. Get you, your spouse, and your family rapture ready. You'll be eternally glad you did!

Ephesians 1:4–6 The Lord has chosen you in Him before the foundation of the world that you should be holy and without blame before Him in love.

Psalm 69: 17 Hide not your face from me, Lord, speedily deliver me from my troubles.

(33)
The Beast 666 Computer

As the saying goes, "Nothing in the imagination of man can exceed the reality of life." But what lies in the deep, dark recesses of man's mind when it comes to mind control may soon surface.

"Black psychiatry" is a science involved in developing electronic techniques to manipulate a person, people, or nation to do whatever is electronically programmed into them. This goes far beyond hypnosis.

For example, you can ask the "Beast 666 Computer" about any person on the planet, and it can pull up information as to where the person lives, his or her occupation, his likes or dislikes, as well as his words and past deeds. The computer pictorially zooms in on him while showing the information. And now they are even working on electronically depicting one's thoughts. Only Almighty God knows the inner thoughts and what lies deep in one's heart. The Antichrist feverishly works to emulate the ability of God, so he hopes to gain access of one's thought waves via the intervention of the computer.

Now get this. According to some unsubstantiated sources, the Beast 666 Computer can potentially make a person do whatever it commands. The computer can make a person rob a bank, have sex, or even kill.

In essence, if you asked the Beast 666 Computer how to

start a conflict or war between two people or two countries, the computer will spill out a plan needed to manipulate the cause and the desired results.

This all sounds like science fiction, but this state-of-art technology is kept so secret as not to alarm the general public—until the right, ripe, satanic time.

With God's divine help, man creates these electronic devices, while unknowingly being deceived by Satan into letting him take control of the computer. Now, let it be understood that Almighty God is always in control. He is millions and millions of times brighter and more lucent than any mechanical/electronic computer. God watches and, in fact, allows all this to happen and come to pass in accordance to His own heavenly atomic clock, which is ticking to the precise time of His return.

The Beast 666 Computer is located in three places. Unofficially, one computer center is in Alaska; one is located in Johannesburg, South Africa; and the other is placed in Australia.

Why those three places? Because those three perfectly, computer-placed spots form a triangle on the earth and fall exactly in line with the occurring forces of the planet.

These three computer centers can pictorially zero in on any one spot on the earth, listen to two human voices, and determine what language is being spoken. It can then transmit an electronic response to make one or both people reply as the computer commands, without their even suspecting what they said or did.

The question is, can the Beast 666 Computer turn thousands and thousands of people into mind-controlled slaves?

It is affirmed that the Beast 666 Computer operates by assigning an eighteen-track digital number to each person. For example, the eighteen computer code numbers are 666 + 110 (which is the code for the United States) … other three digits for other countries) + three-digit phone area code + Social Security number (or prescribed digits for other countries) --- and "bingo" you are on the Beast 666 Computer.

Whenever you use your credit card, you can be sure the transaction is recorded on the Beast 666 Computer. Man has no idea of what he has embarked upon via the computer. He feels as if he is in control, but in reality (I should say spiritually), many are mind-controlled slaves by powers and principalities far beyond his realization.

The Beast 666 Computer operates on an individual's brain waves. The four basic types of brain waves by which the mind operates electronically, either by digital or analog means, are --- alpha, beta, delta, and theta. And that is how the Beast

666 Computer is potentially able to tap in and pick up one's thoughts electronically.

Big brother is now here!

Just how and when the Lord will return and intervene by taking us up and out of this mind-controlled environment has to be near at hand. And those left behind on earth will experience three and one-half years of bliss ... followed by three and one-half years of brutality of apocalyptic proportions.

Pray now that the Lord forgives you of your past sins. Accept Jesus as your Lord and Savior, and ask for His Holy Spirit to imbue you with His born-again spirit. Be rapture ready.

Remember that the pig always returns to the mud. Be not that pig. Rid yourself of bad habits and those who misled you. But do try to help others find the Lord. By doing so, it will cover a multitude of your own sins.

Can the Beast 666 Computer eventually read your mind? It's a possibility. But there is nothing it can do about it. Once you are born again, you are under the Alpha and Omega (the beginning and the end) protective umbrella of the Lord Jesus Christ.

Proverbs 18:10 The name of the Lord is a strong tower; the righteous run into it and are safe.

(34)
One World Currency

THE ANTICHRIST NEEDS ONE WORLD currency to control the people's food, finances and banking system. Once he establishes this universal currency, he can place the electronic implant in the forehead or hand of each person to know how, what, when, where, why and from whom that person purchased any goods.

Satan is well aware that even Jesus had a traitor in his midst. Being such a psychopathic deceiver himself, Satan's paranoia will run rampant in uncovering anyone who can somehow thwart his ruler ship. So, it will be imperative that the Antichrist electronically controls and reviews people's finances and everyday living via the computer.

And knowing also that the Lord God knows not only what people say and do but also what is in their thoughts, Satan (who thrives on emulating God) will work his "Black Psychology" computer wizardry (as well as his demons) to try to uncover even the thoughts of individuals in some way.

Many world economists see in the distant future, in which individual national currencies will be merged into one worldwide currency. Electronically, mankind now has the capability to do this without causing massive devaluation for one country and hyperinflation in another during the switch over.

In today's world marketplace, the U.S. dollar and the European euro are the two main units of world currency. In December 2006, the euro passed the U.S. dollar in the combined value of cash in circulation.

A global currency called either the "earth unit" or the "terra," controlled by a central bank, could possibly satisfy individuals, corporations, governments, and other huge organizations. However, no global currency has yet to be established because of political, economic, and cultural differences. For example, the Islamic faith does not believe in charging interest.

Here are a few of the reasons world economists advocate one world currency:

* Eliminate transaction costs from trading one currency to another.
* Eliminate the risk associated with third-world currency failures.
* Eliminate the need for countries to have currency reserves.
* Eliminate the change of value in currencies.
* Eliminate the need of the multitude of national interest rates.
* Eliminate cash to stop robberies of individuals, stores, homes, and banks.

With one world currency, there is only one interest rate, which can be lowered or raised depending on what country slipped into a recession or inflation. If such a currency is found acceptable by all nations of the world, then that currency will undoubtedly be backed by gold, as gold neither rusts nor decays.

To keep a level economic playing field, no one person can use gold as a means of purchasing power. Gold will only be used by the people as an ornament, for industrial or electronic use, or in other uses serving mankind's needs.

While this one world currency sounds economically good to the ears of mankind, Satan has other financial, slave-controlling ideas for the world's population. After the one world currency is put into effect, the Antichrist will demand that each person receive the electronic 666 implant in his forehead or hand as a means of determining who bought what, where, when, and why. Supermarkets, banks, credit cards, and other institutions already have the means to put this into effect.

With this kind of global central-banking system, Satan's

Beast 666 Computer can cut off the food and other human needs to any one individual, company, or country that fails to follow his hell-bent demands.

Controlling the global currency, then, is one more step Satan will use to pied piper people to his way of living. Those who were not taken up in the preceding rapture of the antichrist can only get to heaven by martyrdom. By not accepting the 666 implant, they will either starve to death or be killed by the followers of Satan.

The world as we now know it will be taken over by Satan and his diabolical demons. The demons, too, will inform the Antichrist as to who is a true follower of Satan. A knock on a person's door will fill him with unbelievable fear.

One has to ask, "Is that what you want?"

If not, immediately ask Almighty God for His forgiveness of your past and present sins, accept Jesus as your Lord and Savior, do not go back to your old unrighteous ways, and get yourself rapture ready. For time is drawing nigh!

1 Timothy 6:10 For the love of money is the root of all evil; which coveted after causes people to err from their faith, and pierce themselves with many sorrows.

(35)
One World Religion

A RECENT SURVEY EXPOSED THE fact that 50 percent of the Christian leaders do not think that Jesus Christ is the Messiah. With that kind of mind-boggling disbelief, is it any wonder that the world is slowly eroding away from Christian principles?

Located in the politically based United Nations is what it called a spiritual equivalent to Christianity called the United Religions Initiative (URI). A charter-writing process is under way to formalize this spiritual empire. Some of the faiths that have gathered for the UR are various Christian denominations, Islam, Buddhism, Hinduism, Judaism, and Sikhism. The organizers of the URI are traveling through India, the Middle East, and Europe seeking spiritual leaders from a multitude of various faiths.

The wrong vision of the URI is to make people feel safe, to create a world where people respect and honor each other, a world where global goodness exists. A plan of action, with a timetable, was set up to allow people from different countries, cultures, religions, and economic backgrounds to gather and shape the safety of the world's population.

One of the main propositions of the URI is that there are many ways to heaven. This doctrine opens the door to the many religious faiths that run contrary to Jesus, who says, "I am the way; the only way to the Father in heaven."

In essence, the URI will be under the shadowing auspices of the United Nations, a government with a political policy with one singular goal in mind, and that is, a one-world government controlled by them.

Psalm 1:1 Blessed is the man or woman who does not walk or adhere to the counsel of the ungodly.

All countries or governments want, in one way or another, to have absolute political control. They feel as if their methodology is the best way to meet the global needs of the people. Without their knowing it consciously, gaining world political control is, in essence, the best way to suit their own personal and mega-political needs.

But all governments are slowly falling prey to the eventual takeover by satanic forces. Day by day, step by step, one congressional and judicial law after another will eventually find world governments subserviently standing outside the door of Satan.

Again, this is not to say that the Lord God is unaware of all this, for He has brought about all this. He has hooked the world governments along with Satan and his hoard of demons to this very spot and time in history. While the element of time and chance are within the framework of life with mankind, it is not that way with Almighty God. He is in absolute control of all people and things, as heaven is His throne and the earth is His footstool.

In conclusion, the URI do not place their ultimate hope in Almighty God or in the divine grace of Jesus Christ. They, instead, offer an individual, earthly utopia of universal peace and goodwill offered to those who join their spiritual allegiance.

The URI openly emphasize that their earthly transcendental, metaphysical philosophy is not in any way anti-Christ in origin, even though they spiritually turn their back on Christ. This is a willful spiritual blindness—eyes that do not see, and ears that do not hear—all brought about by the deceptive perception of Satan, for the URI is nothing more than an emblematic arm of the United Nations.

Be not fooled by the URI's claim to have goodness preempt Christ's umbrella of grace. Did not Jesus say, "At the end times, if God does not intervene, even the very elect will be deceived?"

Yes, time is drawing nigh!

1 Peter 1:7 The trial of your faith will be tried like gold with fire that might be found the praise, honor and glory in the reappearing of Jesus Christ.

(36)
A One-World Military:
United Nations, NATO

NATO, THE NORTH ATLANTIC TREATY Organization, began in 1949 and is headquartered in Brussels, Belgium.

Where else? Hope you are getting the picture.

Members of NATO agree that an attack on any country in Europe or North America shall be considered an attack against all of them.

Here's the catch.

An attack on America does not necessarily mean that all of the NATO countries will militarily join in against the attacker. Some countries (regardless of the seriousness of the situation) may deem it necessary to use diplomacy to try and settle the matter, although a war may be raging potentially out of control.

NATO consists of twenty-eight countries: Albania, Belgium, Bulgaria, Canada, Croatia, Czech Republic, Denmark, Estonia, France, Germany, Greece, Hungary, Iceland, Italy, Latvia, Lithuania, Luxembourg, Netherlands, Norway, Poland, Portugal, Romania, Slovakia, Slovenia, Spain, Turkey, United Kingdom, and United States. The Soviet Union was rejected by NATO out of fear that its motive was to weaken the alliance.

The pieces of the puzzle fit together very nicely when you see where NATO falls under the jurisdiction of the United Nations to form a global military force.

Now the question is, with all these countries (with the possibility that more will join) banned together to instill worldwide peace, who will they have to fight?

Of course, there is Russia, China, and some rogue third-world countries as well as world terrorists with whom to deal. But say, somehow, those countries become members. Then what?

The "then what" is --- well, no one is left to fight. And, if there is no one to fight, then why have a NATO force?

Now we get to the interesting part.

Could the NATO military force ultimately be a forceful arm of the United Nations in order to muscle countries into its way of thinking—or else!

Does it not say somewhere not to put ultimate power in a good man's hands, let alone an evil person?

Now, I am sure that the United Nations with its NATO force is presently planning nothing but good and peaceful things for the people in this world.

But, does it realize that its good intentions may someday be taken over by the Antichrist?

The Antichrist has to have under his domain (1) the banking currency system, (2) the government, (2) the media, (4) the judicial system, (5) the religious order, (6) the Beast 666 Computer, and (7) the military (police force) to quell any uprisings by unsatisfied countries or individuals.

Everything seems to be falling in fast order for a one-world-order Antichrist, especially with all data and authority being centered in one location: Brussels, Belgium.

One thousand human years is like a day to the Lord God. Hmmm, let's see, according to the Lord's time, that means it has been about two days since the Lord Jesus was here, three days since David, four days since Abraham, and I figure another two days since Adam and Eve. That makes approximately six days or so since the beginning of mankind --- going on 7.

You see, we humans think the Lord's return is taking too long. Well, many beg to disagree with you. For time is drawing nigh!

Anytime now, in a blink of the eye, the followers and believers of Christ will be taken up into heaven. And all that will be left here on earth are the demons, who will unmercifully plague everyone left on the globe. For, like Satan, they hate mankind.

Be not deceived. Get yourself rapture ready!

Proverbs 20:18 Every purpose is established by counsel, and with good advice make war.

(37)
One World Bank

THE WORLD BANK, LOCATED IN Washington DC, is a family of five international organizations formalized by the United Nations in 1945 for economic development and to eliminate poverty in the world. The president of the United States, the largest shareholder, nominates the president of the World Bank for a five-year term.

While the prestige of the World Bank is, for the most part, held high by neighboring and joining countries, it is not incorruptible. The former president of the World Bank resigned under some signs of disrepute. The World Bank works on stopping embezzlement and other forms of corruption. Hiring people not capable of properly fulfilling their employment obligations is also wrong.

No country is forced to borrow money from the World Bank. And the World Bank does provide loans as well as grants to those who need it. Loans made to third-world or other poor countries are made at below- market interest rates.

The World Bank was first established to rebuild war-torn Europe following World War II. The first loan of $250 million dollars was given to France.

Regardless of the good done by the World Bank, some countries feel that it can become too imperialistic. It takes only a few people in control to make this imperialistic viewpoint become a stark reality.

If and when the world starts to believe the media that cash is too tempting for crooks and other vandals, today's currency can easily be transformed into a mere credit card, which most institutions now accept and use.

The next step will be that the card can easily be compromised, and something else has to take its place to assure that individual users are not duped.

As we have recently witnessed, the bankruptcy of the top investment banks and local banks indicates the flimsy, insubstantial monetary weakness of our present banking system. The government is subsidizing these banks and simultaneously taking control of them.

One wonders if there is any correlation of the United States putting "In God We Trust" on the edge of their coin (rather than on the face) to the Dow plunge of 777 points in one day (which, incidentally, is the number of the Lord God). And now we have our monetary system on the financial edge. One can only imagine what will happen to the U.S. economy when the secular humanists decide to take "In God We Trust" entirely off all currency. For you see, the only way any nation's currency is valid and safe is when it is backed by faith in God.

All this leads eventually to the Lord allowing an international banking system that can then easily be taken over by Satan. The one person who will then step in at the right moment will be the Antichrist. He has a plan by which no one can steal your money or credit card. He will suggest (during his second three and one-half year period of control) that you simply put a tiny 666 chip in your forehead or hand for true identity to buy or trade items.

And presto! Just like that, the user has lost his transport to heaven, for no person who has that 666 chip can enter heaven.

Many theologians tell you this much. Before that 666 chip is put into people, those followers and believers in Jesus Christ, the only begotten Son of Almighty God, will be taken up in Jesus' rapture. And the only way to heaven afterward is by martyrdom.

So, get yourself ready. Time is truly drawing nigh. It is never too late to ask the Lord God for forgiveness and accept Jesus Christ as your Lord and Savior.

It is your rapture ticket to heaven!

Matthew 25:14–30 If you are afraid of losing your money and hide it (without even bearing interest) the Lord will condemn you and cast you into darkness.

(38)
One World Judicial System

THE INTERNATIONAL COURT OF JUSTICE, or ICJ (also known as the World Court) is located in The Hague, Netherlands. It is the judicial arm of the United Nations court and was established in 1945 by UN charter.

There are fifteen judges on the ICJ, who are elected to a nine-year term and may be reelected, at the most, for two other terms. Elections take place every three years, with one-third of the judges retiring or reelected each time to assure continuation of the court. No two judges can be of the same nationality.

Besides the ICJ, there is the International Criminal Court (ICC). The ICC was established in 2002 to prosecute individuals (not states) for genocide, crimes against humanity, war crimes, and crimes of aggression. It is worth noting that the ICC is legally and functionally independent of the United Nations. And the ICC has its own police force and works side by side with national authorities.

The ICJ and the ICC are basically world courts that can conceivably establish criteria as to what constitutes a crime in their particular courtroom. Their criteria for the basis of a crime can have devastating effects on individuals who knowingly or unknowingly fall within their jurisdiction.

The question is when, where, and how far can the ICJ and the ICC overstep the judicial authority of a given state or country?

We have witnessed cases in which leaders of countries are considered as having trespassed international law and have paid dearly with their life.

But, and this is a big but, what if the ICJ and the ICC decide to make a given individual in, say America, surrender himself or herself to their judicial demands for what they, in their viewpoint, consider corrupt or cataclysmic actions toward humanity? For example, if America makes a preemptive attack on another country based on its possession of and plan to use WMDs and none are found (having been hidden by the warmonger) the ICJ and the ICC, if they deems so, can consider the preemptive attack a criminal violation of international law and bring the alleged intruders to stand before the international court of law.

The point here is once an evil force overtakes the ICJ or the ICC, all hell can break loose in the judicial system.

Have we set up the embryonic world court judicial system that can some day be controlled by Satan? And with its own police force, there will be little one can do other than succumb to the judicial demands of the ICC or the ICJ.

It does not take too much stretch of the imagination to see where the world judicial system does provide world security from despots, but it is just one more step Satan can use to control the world's population through judiciary means with the needed police and military force to back it up.

It is told, and I think you can sense it, time is drawing nigh.

There may be a time when the World Court can eventually be everything *but* judicial.

John 7:24 Judge not by appearance, but judge righteous judgment.

(39)
One World Media

At the end of World War II, 80 percent of the media in the country was privately owned. Today, just the opposite is true. A few media corporations, even if privately owned, now control over 80 percent of the media outlets.

This centralized control over our worldwide media gives a few people enormous power. The real problem is that some corporations, for the most part, have no heart. They exist on profit levels (like 15 percent to 20 percent at least) to satisfy Wall Street investors. What this means is advertisers who financially stake the media giants can, at times, get away with murder.

Take the example of the tobacco industry. The media giants knew fifty years ago that tobacco was injurious to one's health. But the tobacco advertising revenue clouded the minds of the media moguls. So, while the dangers had been known for years, it was only relatively recently that they came to light.

Moreover, people across the planet earth need unbiased information in order to make intelligent decisions about their choices of political candidates, global warming, terrorist threats, gas and oil prices, housing and mortgage rates, dangerous situations, and a host of other important life-saving issues. If a given media giant (be it newspaper, TV, Internet, or whatever) is slanting its reports in favor of what benefits them and not others, you can see the danger for the world's population.

In 1953, fifty corporations controlled the media outlets in the United States. Today, more than one in five Internet users log in on AOL, which until December 2009, was part of Time Warner, the world's largest media corporation.

The increasing control of the media by a handful of corporations means that they can control what the global market reads, sees, hears—and believes.

Whenever worldwide economic interests are at stake, the media giants can heavily weight the stations with news contrary to the good of the people but, simultaneously, for the profitable good of themselves.

As you can visualize, media pertaining to world economic and political factors can easily be distorted if, someday, it is completely controlled by satanic forces.

Correct, timely information is crucial in today's world. Deceptively motivated media, in such situations, can potentially make the people come to extreme and violently wrong global conclusions.

Here's an example. The TV media flashes that hundreds of gay couples are being married. Hey, the population of the United States is three hundred four million. Such TV coverage makes it appear that marriage by gay couples is on the rise. Again, only about 2.3 percent of the U.S. population is gay. So why and how is such a small percentage of the country controlling the thoughts and wavelengths of national and international TV?

The question is, who will eventually take over the world's media system?

Do you not see where time is drawing nigh for the Antichrist to step in and via shareholder monopoly or pure military power grab hold of the one world media system to have the people see, read, and hear what he has to tell them.

Look here. If a thousand years of human life is only one day to the Lord, the same is true with Satan. He has deceived and monopolized the media in fifty human years (which is only minutes of his time). Having the majority of the media in the hands of a few corporations, Satan (via the Antichrist) can eventually take it over in one fell swoop. That is how fast Satan is working and how short your time is to spiritually prepare yourself to be under Christ's umbrella of grace.

Yep, by taking over the world's media, one more step is taken by Satan for world domination.

Now are you getting the emotional vibes to get Jesus' rapture ready?

Ephesians 4:29 Let no corrupt communications proceed from your mouth; only that which is good and edifies the grace unto the hearers..

(40)
One World Government

THE NEW WORLD ORDER, NWO (one world government), is best described as a world superpower designed to secure and maintain global peace. As evidenced by many world thought leaders, the New World Order is a step-by-step takeover of the courts, media, banking, religion, military, and government through the electronic wizardry of today's modernized computer to dominate every aspect of the world's population. The NWO will become the global superpower, giving some sovereignty (but not much) to countries throughout the world.

No one government has ever taken over the entire world. At one time, the British Empire controlled one-quarter of the world's surface and one-third of the world's population.

Other world organizations set up for potential or eventual global control include, the World Health Organization, the

International Labor Organization, the International Monetary Fund, the International Telecommunications Union, the United Religions Initiative, the International Court of Justice, the International Criminal Court, and international military forces, such as NATO.

Allegations are pouring in that national politicians are secretly creating this NWO, which will replace the sovereignty of the national governments. This will be accomplished by social engineering and fear-provoking political propaganda, global monetary failure, and other preset international fiascos.

The NWO, sounds an efficient and effective way to bring about world peace and prosperity, but its proponents have not the slightest clue as to who is behind this global peace plan.

It is very plain for those who are spiritually connected to the Lord God to see where the NWO is headed. And it is right into the hands of the Antichrist. Satan's subtle and deceptive means to gain control has one purpose in mind: to suppress and enslave the world's population to his way of thinking, speaking, and living. But first, he must set up all the international organizations to be electronically controlled by his Beast 666 Computer network.

Again, the basic international organizations Satan needs to have set up before he introduces the Antichrist are the media, the courts, the banks, the military, the religious institutions, and the electronic surveillance and account system of the computer.

The question is --- are the international organizations presently in place?

Can they be easily overtaken if some catastrophic terrorist situation takes place around the world, and one person—like the Antichrist—announces that he can bring about world peace?

Clearly, you can see that people will clamor over anyone who can stop any kind of nuclear detonation and place him in a supreme position as long as he can maintain peace.

From there, you can visualize when you will have three and one-half years of peace and prosperity and then the unchecked mega mania and paranoia of the Antichrist will foment into the next three and one-half years of stark terror.

The question remains, do you want to be taken up by Jesus' rapture before the Antichrist begins his reign?

If the answer is a resounding yes, you need to ask Almighty God immediately for forgiveness of your sins, accept Jesus Christ as your Lord and Savior, and ask for His Holy Spirit to enter your mind, heart, and soul.

Then you are rapture ready!

2 Peter 2:10 The unrighteous lust and despise good government. They are self-willed and speak evil of dignities.

(41)
A Review of Global Constitutional Rights

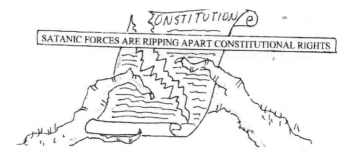

IN MY MIND, I AM grateful not to have the political, judicial, military, religious, monetary, and mass media decisions that many people across the world have in their hands. I feel I would fall far short of their capabilities, so I do not judge their shortcomings or weaknesses in times of emergency or tight decision making.

We all fall short of the glory of God. And we all make grievous mistakes. It is when we know of our evil intentions and work to justify them contrary to God's precepts and commandments that we reap His condemnatory wrath.

At this point in time, I personally feel that the leaders across the world, for the most part, either do not believe there is a Messiah named Jesus and that there is no Antichrist on the horizon, or they are willfully blinded by their zeal in establishing global control for the alleged betterment of mankind.

Many people, in some way, feel that a world order might solve many of the world's wars, monetary problems, judicial decisions, and other workable global situations. But, we do have eyes that see and ears that hear the word of God. Consequently, we know where the one world order road is heading. It is presently on the road to the Antichrist's place of operation. And all roads (media, banking, judicial, military, religion, government, and computer control) seem to be heading to Brussels, Belgium, as part and parcel of the European Union.

In no way is anyone casting political dispersions on Brussels, Belgium, or the European Union. They obviously do not see or believe that the Antichrist can and will deceive them into his submission and control.

Right now, the national governments across the world are under legal and financial tsunamis by secular humanists who want to change the way the world thinks and lives. The three basic governing laws of any judicial court are (1) writ of habeas corpus, (2) ex post facto, and (3) due process of law.

Leaders of countries want to remove the power of the federal courts to use the writ of habeas corpus on foreign citizens held by them on suspicions of committing acts of terrorism in their respective country. They also want to remove from federal courts ex post facto, the right of enacting or operating retroactively.

While this might seem to be a good idea to leaders who are striving to offset terrorism in their country, can you not see where this is an ideal judicial tool for the eventual use of the Antichrist? A judicial tool to call anyone in on suspicion, who will have no recourse under writ of habeas corpus or ex post facto.

The onslaught against church versus state is nothing more than a ploy. The Constitution can only be read by using one's faith as a guideline. The secular humanists know this. And subtly, they hope the federal, state, and local courts do not know or understand this. You see, at one time, in order to be an attorney or judge, you had to also have a theological degree. That way, the judges and lawyers would make decisions about law and the Constitution by using their <u>faith</u> as well as their <u>legal</u> mind. The two go together inexplicably.

An example of this is when the U.S. Supreme Court decided in Roe v. Wade that a fetus is not a person based on the Constitution. You see, you cannot take someone's life unless he receive his right of due process guaranteed under the <u>Fifth</u> and <u>Fourteenth</u> Amendments. Due process of law means exactly that. A person must have a judicial hearing. But, the fetus does not get a judicial hearing, as it was determined by the Court that the fetus is not a person based purely on the Constitution (not integrating the element of faith in the Bible; see Jeremiah 1:5).

If you look in the first chapter of the book of Jeremiah, you will see that the Lord says in Jeremiah 1:5, "'Before I formed you in the womb, I knew you.'" And the Lord God treats all alike. So, if the fetus is a person before it is in the womb, how much more of a person once is it in the womb? But today's secular, humanistic judges do not use faith in making judicial decisions, only their secular interpretation of the law and the Constitution to hide their despicable judicial decisions.

Again, we must emphasize that, for the most part, the national and world judges, attorneys, politicians, bankers, media moguls, and religious leaders are doing the right things. And their vision of a one-world government has some merit in its inception, but the eventual outcome is easily conceived, as Satan has his eyes on world control.

Satan imitates all that Almighty God creates and does. God has Christ. Satan has the Antichrist. God has the Holy Spirit. Satan has the beast. God has His angels. Satan has his angels (demons).

So you see, Satan is setting the world stage for his Antichrist and the beast to take over all for his domain.

Our forefathers knew of the evil spiritual powers and principalities that exist in the world, so they dovetailed theology with law in the belief that good spiritual men and women would use their faith as well as law when making governmental and judicial decisions about the Constitution.

And would not Satan like to get rid of the right to bear arms in the Second Amendment of the Constitution? That way, he can protect and make sure there is no uprising against the Antichrist.

It is guarantee that every time you hear of a given city, state, or country banning the right of its citizens to bear arms, you will find wholesale robberies taking place, as the people cannot properly defend themselves.

Secular, activist judges do not use faith in today's judicial decisions. And woe, woe, woe unto them when the Lord God renounces them on Judgment Day!

My prayers are for the leaders across the globe, for their job is one few can fulfill. But my prayers are also for the readers of this book to get ready. Time really is drawing nigh!

Let's conclude with this plea unto the readers of this book: bow down and ask the Lord God to forgive you of your unrighteous thoughts, words, and deeds, for time is truly drawing nigh. Get yourself Jesus' rapture ready. He is coming soon!

Psalm 37:31 The law of the Lord is in his heart; therefore his steps shall not slide.

(42)
Shortage of Oil

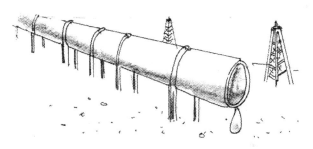

THE SUPPLY OF OIL HAS peaked. It is in depletion. Approximately 98 percent of the countries now producing oil are near their production peak.

Our reliance on tar sands, shale, coal-to-liquids, hydrogen, bio-diesel, and ethanol fuels do nothing but lose precious scientific time for us. It appears that our only opportunity to sustain life, as we know, it is with solar energy. Someday we may be riding in solar-powered vehicles on fixed guide ways.

The cost of a barrel of oil has risen during the following crisis periods:

- 1967 Six Day War, where Israel was attacked by Arab nations.
- 1973 Syria and Egypt attacked Israel, and the United States aided Israel.

- 1979 Iranian crisis, when U.S. hostages were held in Iran.
- 1990 Gulf War.
- 2003 War in Iraq.

It is no secret that a terrorist attack or military coup on Middle East oil facilities would cause global shortages and starvation in many parts of the world.

Presently, the world consumes approximately 42 billion barrels of oil per year. Mankind uses 1.2 cubic miles of oil per year. It was estimated in 2006 that only 32 cubic miles of oil is readily available. It has peaked!

If progress cannot be sustained in society because of the lack of energy from the oil-producing countries, civilization as we now know it will go into a cataclysmic economic chaos.

As we are witnessing, the prices of oil and its refining process to create gasoline has risen dramatically, part of which is the result of political collusion. But is this the birth pains of peaked oil?

Right now, the world's population is 6.5 billion. It was 1.6 billion in 1900, 1 billion in 1800, and 500 million in 1500. The exponential figures of population growth alone make it very difficult to maintain the energy to sustain life as we know it.

At $4 a gallon for gasoline, many companies will be laying off workers and charging more for their services or product lines (worth noting again is that gas prices and the economy simmer down after major elections and other political factions cease). Nevertheless, oil energy as we know it is depleting, and prices will increase due to the law of supply and demand. If a barrel of oil reaches $300 a barrel, a complete shutdown of the global economy could occur, and countries will be at war to see who can take over the oil-producing fields and refineries.

The eight hundred-mile Alaska Pipeline, costing $8 billion to build, runs south to the Gulf of Alaska, where it supplies the refineries in the forty-eight states below. It produces 2.1 million gallons of oil a day. America alone uses nearly 10 billion barrels of oil a year.

It is important to remember that oil refineries produce gasoline, kerosene, heating oil, natural gas, plastic derivatives, as well as a host of direly needed products to sustain life.

It does not take much to connect the dots as to how shaky and dire the situation is with the world's energy. And the carbon dioxide (CO_2) emitted from the oil-derived products may be causing alarming global warming.

The question is, what can we do? We must firmly believe that as a nation and world, we must pray for Almighty God's intervention. And get Congress to drill oil wells and build refineries immediately, as we search for the answer in solar power.

2 Samuel 22:22–23 God is my strength and power, and He makes the way perfect for all who trust in Him.

(43)
Nuclear Power

NUCLEAR FUSION ENERGY IS RELEASED when atoms are combined or fused together to form a larger atom. This is how the sun produces energy.

Nuclear fission occurs when atoms are split to form smaller atoms that release energy. Nuclear power plants use nuclear fission to produce energy.

The fuel mostly used by nuclear power plants is uranium. A certain kind of uranium, U-235, is used, as its atoms easily split apart. When the neutron hits the uranium atom, a heat chain reaction is caused, releasing heat and radiation. The process repeats itself over and over again. The liquid around the uranium pipes heats up, producing steam that, in turn, drives the force to turn the gigantic turbines, thereby producing electrical energy.

Presently, the world's 439 nuclear plants provide around 15 percent of the world's electricity. While nuclear power provides 19 percent of U.S. electricity, in France, it provides 78 percent.

The discrepancy between the use of nuclear power in the United States and France is due, in part, to its controversial nature. Electricity was generated the first time via nuclear power in 1951, at an experimental station in Idaho. At this early stage of nuclear power, controversy was over the use of hydrogen fusion or uranium fission.

In 1970 and 1980, falling oil prices made the cost of building nuclear power plants financially unfeasible, and vocal environmental concerns hindered their construction.

Even so, as of 2007, the United States with their nuclear power plants have accumulated more than fifty thousand metric tons of spent nuclear fuel from nuclear reactors. Much of the storage of nuclear waste is to be directed to the Yucca Mountains in Nevada, where, after ten thousand years of radioactive decay, the nuclear wastes no longer poses a threat to public health or safety.

The Union of Concerned Scientists (UCS), founded in 1969 by faculty and students at MIT, formed the organization to turn away from military technology and place scientific emphasis on environmental and social problems. The UCS supports wind, solar, and geothermal energy sources.

It is worth noting that nuclear energy is safe as far as the greenhouse effect is concerned; however, it is still too costly, and there is no solution for the safe storage of the abundance of nuclear waste. Moreover, there is danger that nuclear waste can get into the hands of terrorists to make dirty bombs.

Another energy source will be needed to replace the depleted oil reserves, and time is running out fast. The time projection for the necessity of a new energy source is thirty to fifty years.

If a new energy source is not discovered and put into place soon, there will be economic chaos throughout the world, as hunger and starvation will be so rampant that one's imagination cannot begin to depict the savagery of it.

This is one more example of where Satan will potentially introduce the Antichrist and the beast to provide three and one-half years of world peace and prosperity (followed by three and one-half years of stark terror) by achieving some sort of energy relief during this cataclysmic period in time.

No one knows the day or the hour, but you can tell by certain signs, be they business, economic, energy, weather, or political, that a worldwide satanic change is about to take place.

Revelation 20:10 And Satan that deceived the people was cast into the lake of fire and brimstone, where the beast and the Antichrist are, and shall be tormented day and night forever and ever.

(44)
Lack of Common Sense

WHILE THE WORLD IS SKYROCKETING in intelligence, it is deep-sea diving in common sense. Many of the scientists, politicians, judges, businesspeople, theologians, and thought leaders have profound learning and creative intellect … but they fall far short of good judgment when applying their creative capacity for the benefit of mankind.

When applied correctly, common sense is practical, sensible, well-founded, sound, judicially solid, prudent, logical, and free from vulgarities.

Common sense is, in essence, nothing more than following each and every precept of the Lord God's scriptures for thinking, speaking, and applying conceptual data in making any kind of decision. Now that may sound too religious, devout, or holy to many of the readers, but it is well known that it also sounded too theological to Satan.

So, you have to make your decision. Do you operate your life or your job with a secular, humanistic viewpoint, or do you pray for divine guidance and stay within the commandments of God when applying your skills?

The Lord God does not look for great ideas, skills, or talents when selecting people to assure that His people do not perish. Instead, He uses those who have the great likeness and the courageous obedience of His only begotten Son, Jesus Christ, when seeking people for important positions in life.

For you see, truth is not what we think it is; it is what God says it is!

Bear in mind also, that Almighty God never compromises truth, and we are never to stop trying.

It is with psychological assurance and testament that whatever "act" you commit, it is the offspring from the very root of your most inner thoughts. So, be careful of your thoughts and words, for from there leaps forward what you will actually do and become in life.

You have seen people who have not used common sense in certain situations. This has been true from your family members, neighbors, politicians, pastors, professors, doctors, as well as yourself. In essence, if you lie, steal, swear, cheat, or do anything contrary to the will of God, you are not using common sense.

So, the secret to having common sense is to stay tucked in the word of God. Then and only then will your intelligence follow a straight, commonsense plumb line. You can tell from the inner peace of your mind and heart if you are playing on an even playing field of life.

Where are you now in life? Are you using common sense in whatever role you are playing?

If you see others getting away with wrong words or actions, do not imitate their behavior, for they may have been given over by the Lord, or they may not even be of the seed of God.

You must not care who, how, when, where, why, what, or if … it is up to you, at that very instance, to use your own common sense (truth) when making intelligent decisions.

So, dust off the past mistakes. Start using common sense. Start putting God first and yourself second, and you will rise from the bottom to the top of your life.

Psalm 94:10–12 The Lord knows the thoughts of man are vanity. But blessed is the man whom the Lord chastens and corrects, for that man will have knowledge and know right from wrong.

(45)
Lack of Clean Drinking Water

ACCORDING TO THE LATEST SCIENTIFIC studies, 2.6 billion people (over 40 percent of the world's population) do not have sanitation facilities and clean drinking water. Such unsanitary situations (mostly in Africa and Asia) cause disease to spread, killing millions of children. Diarrhea currently takes the lives of 1.5 million children per year.

The world's water crisis is one of the largest health issues of our time. Desalinization plants are beginning to stabilize previously devastated areas of the world's drinking water, along with the technology to get water from air to help the arid regions of the Earth.

The world's water crisis is one of the largest health issues of our time. As an example, if the earth's water fit in a gallon jug, only one tablespoon of water would be available for drinking purposes.

This safe drinking water problem is not just confined to one particular region of the earth, as one-third of the earth's population is presently water stressed. And this number is expected to rise dramatically over the next two decades --- although desalinization can provide relief where and when political and expenditures permit it.

The next war may very well be over water, not oil.

While water is renewable, it is also finite. We are now using about half of the safe water available on planet earth. Agriculture uses about 70 percent, followed by industry and individuals, all of which is increasing almost exponentially.

Scientific studies show that the availability of safe water for agriculture, industry, and individual use will pass the "available point" around the year 2025. When and if this happens, there will be a tremendous need in this decade to cooperate and share the water in rivers, ponds, lakes, and wells, as well as the technology for desalinization and getting water from with neighbors, counties, states, and countries. Thought leaders, politicians, scientists, businesspeople, and others feel there is a need for international intervention to stabilize and equalize the distribution of safe water in the near future.

Have you ever been so thirsty you feel the intense parched lips and dry mouth, and there is no water around? How you yearn for just one drink, just one tiny drop of water.

Theologians assure you that those left here on this earth, when Satan takes over the water supply will bow down and do anything (including implanting his infamous 666 on one's forehead or right hand) for that clenching taste of water.

So, you can see where this is another example where the one world government is taking center stage in the management of many areas of the globe.

Again, many are beginning to tell you to get ready for Jesus' rapture, for *He* is the living waters. Yes, time truly is drawing nigh.

Psalm 33:6–7, 22 By the Word of God the heavens were made. He gathers the waters of the sea together as a heap, and He lays it in the depth of His storehouse Oh, Lord, let your mercy be upon us, as we accordingly hope in you.

(46)
Global Warming

GLOBAL WARMING REFERS TO AN average increase in the earth's temperature that, in turn, causes a change in the climate. The earth has warmed about 1 degree Fahrenheit in the past one hundred years.

The rise in temperature is caused by certain gases in the atmosphere, such as carbon dioxide, nitrogen oxide, and methane, trapping energy from the sun. This is called the greenhouse effect, as it equates to what happens in an actual greenhouse, whereby, the heat from the sun enters through the glass panes and warms the plants inside.

The atmosphere surrounds the earth like the glass windows of a greenhouse. The sun's rays travel through the atmosphere and heat the earth. Then the same rays travel back into space, cooling the Earth. When those same rays cannot travel back into space because of the excess carbon dioxide, nitrogen oxide, and methane gases trapped in the atmosphere, the earth's surface can become over warmed.

You can see this happening in desert areas. Since there are usually no clouds there, the sun's rays travel back into space very easily, making the arid land extremely hot during the day yet very cold at night. In some regions of the earth, many clouds trap the sun's rays from returning into space, and those regions of the earth remain warmer at night.

When the sun's rays cannot travel back into space, this causes glacier melting, rise in ocean levels, droughts in various regions of the earth, an overabundance of rain elsewhere, decimation of plant and animal life, and a spread of diseases.

Oceans cover 70 percent of the earth's surface, land covers 27 percent, and ice_covers the remaining 3 percent. High tide has risen six to eight inches since the start of the Industrial Revolution, some two hundred years ago. Some believe this increased emphasis and industrialization caused the beginning of the greenhouse effect.

If global warming exists, the earth will have heat waves, rise in sea level, coastal flooding, Arctic and Antarctic warming, glaciers melting, early spring arrival, downpours, heavy snow, droughts, fires, the spread of disease—and pandemonium within the human population due to the lack of safe water, food, and daily necessities.

The earth is the Lord's footstool. He owns and controls all in, under, over, within, and around the earth. The Lord's angels control the weather, the wind, the tides, and everything else concerning the earth. Yet, there are many people in high office who do not know this, let alone believe it.

Prayer and repentance are needed to keep the world running smoothly. Otherwise, we give ourselves over to the evil powers and principalities whose total aim is the destruction of our very life as we know it.

This earth is an inheritance granted to us by the Lord God. And it is an inheritance to your children and your children's children. It is up to all of us to make sure we keep within the Lord's commandments in order to pass on this spiritual inheritance. However, I wonder about this very seriously, since the government and judicial system are actually making the people take down the Ten Commandments in response to vocal minority requests at the expense of the population's majority of spiritual believers. Will we be able to save the earth if the Ten Commandments are treated so lightly by those who make our laws?

Woe, woe unto you who mock God by voicing against the Ten Commandments and to you who judicially submit to such unrighteous demands. For the fires of hell, filled with sulfuric fumes, may very well lick upward as your reward.

It is never too late to ask Almighty God to free you from such unholy and depraved thinking. Reach out for the God's blessings, not Satan's cursing.

Deuteronomy 11:26–28 "Behold, I set before you this day a blessing or a curse. A blessing if you obey the commandments of the Lord your God, which I command you this day. And a curse if you will not obey the commandments of the Lord your God, and turn away from which I command you this day."

(47)
Worldwide Shortage of Food

TODAY, MORE THAN TWENTY COUNTRIES across the world experience extreme malnutrition. The World Health Organization is very concerned, as patients do not have the strength to fight off and are dying from HIV, pneumonia, measles, malaria, and diarrhea. The H5N1 virus (bird flu) could take hold in those countries, and a pandemic could threaten

The concern is with the weakened health-conditions of the people in these 20 countries; whereby the H5N1 bird flu could take hold there, and a pandemic outbreak could threaten people worldwide.

Opponents to the idea that there is a worldwide food shortage state that the food shortage is a result of social injustice, political posturing, and economic exclusion. Added to this is the fact that about one-third of vegetables and fruits are wasted before they get to distribution points of need because of poorly ventilated storage areas.

In this equation of food need, the world's population doubled from three billion people in 1959 to over six billion in 1999, and it is estimated that three billion more for the year 2042. Isn't it ironic, yet sad, that so much of the world's population suffers the results of overeating while, the other part possibly does not have enough food?

Genetic technologies for breeding food crops can result in improved production of vegetables and fruits, but there is also a scientific need for evidence of the health safety of those modified foods. This "green revolution" can bring about a significant increase in food production, but the fertilizers and pesticides could possibly reduce the life expectancy of the end users.

Ending political intervention in the distribution of food could eliminate many of the poverty traps around the world.

Right now it is stated that 70 percent of the pesticide market is in the hands of six giant agrochemical corporations. And, ten of the biggest food companies account for one-quarter of all the food produced. Also, ten of the largest distribution chains account for one-quarter of all food distribution. Are you getting the picture?

Again, so much of the economy is shrinking into the hands of so few, all of which will easily enable the Antichrist to take command if and when any shortfall occurs in the food distribution chain due to weather, global warming, economic upheaval, energy crisis, or other catastrophic situations.

The quest for food for human survival has been a major preoccupation since the Stone Age. The lack of food is one of the major reasons countries go to war.

The need for food teeters on many variables, but the most important is prayer. It is the Lord God who meets the supply and demand for the world's needs.

Psalm 104:13–14 The Lord waters the hills for the cattle, and herb for the service of man, and He brings forth food out of the earth.

2 Chronicles 1:14 "If my people, who are called by my name, shall humble themselves and pray and seek my face and turn from their wicked ways, then I will hear from them in Heaven and will forgive their sins and will heal their land."

(48)
Disbelief and Disregard of the Scriptures

"In the beginning God created the heaven and the earth. And God said, 'Let there be light.' And there was light."

And in the beginning was the Word, and the Word was with God, and the Word was God.

The Word and the Light became Jesus Christ. For those who follow His words and fall under His light are saved by Father God.

Historically, Jesus was in the world, the very world He helped make for mankind, yet there are those who choose to listen to the words of the world and venture out of the Light and into the shadows of darkness.

We live in a world not just of mere blood and flesh but of angelic beings both good and evil. Does not the Word of God tell you that Satan and his fallen angels were cast unto the earth? And woe, woe unto the people on the earth, for those fallen angels (called demons), are hell-bent on destroying mankind.

Almighty God gave mankind the gift of life and the earth, yet the how, when, where, why, who, and what we do here on earth is up to each one of us individually. We can live a life in the light of goodness or in the darkness of evil.

When we as mankind decide to take down the Ten Commandments, to eliminate any mention of God in the school system, to shy away from the mere mention of Jesus Christ as Lord and Savior of the world, we begin to enter into the shadows of darkness, and we will reap all the destructive chaos that the demons of Satan wait to heap upon us.

Basically, there are three kinds of people. (1) The carnal person who always puts his or her personal appetite and pleasure first. They must get some form of physical, passionate, or satisfy a craving from anything they do. (2) Then there is the ego person, who does things only if it makes him or her look good. Vanity to them is a prize worth possessing. (3) The most enduring, however, is the spirit-filled person, who does something simply and basically because it is the right thing to do.

These three types of people all have one thing in common: self-esteem. Low self-esteem most generally falls under the first two categories. The person with high self-esteem person is the one most likely to do the right thing at the right time.

We all oscillate between the three categories at times, but most generally stay in the spirit-filled person. Where do you situate yourself among the three? God knows. Do you?

The angels of Almighty God thwart the demons of Satan. But we have a choice to allow the angels of God or allow the demons of Satan to intervene in our life.

Amazing how man will use electricity, bulldozers, and other gadgets to help them in life but never begin to really realize how powerful prayer to Almighty God to release His angels can be the major key to accomplishing anything.

Have you ever heard someone say, "Don't preach to me," when anything was mentioned about the scriptures. They have little realization that it was Satan who made them say that. Did not Jesus even say to His disciples, "'Get back from me, Satan,'" when they mentioned something contrary to the word of God.

There are many in the world who are not even of the seed of God, as their unrighteous behavior and their refusal to acknowledge Jesus as their Lord and Savior have given their soul over to Satan.

You see and hear such people in the various media outlets. They make statements that make a straight line crooked, and they equivocate on everything they say.

Be not amazed or dismayed by such people. And follow not their worldly words of advice, for they are in the shadows of darkness.

There will come a day when a generation will fall completely away from the Lord God. The many people still left here on earth who have not accepted Jesus Christ as their Savior and received their spiritual rapture ticket will suffer greatly, as eventual martyrdom is their only and last opportunity to gain access to heaven.

Time is truly drawing nigh. Get yourself Jesus' rapture ready. Many of you will pass away before the rapture. A premature death is, in essence, your individual rapture to heaven or decent into hell. So, be acutely aware, because for each of us, either Jesus or Satan is coming soon. It's your choice!

John 3:3 Verily, verily, I say unto you—except a man be 'born again,' he cannot see the kingdom of heaven.

(49)
Organized and Corporate Crime

PRACTICALLY EVERYONE READS OR HEARS about the criminal who gets caught stealing, corrupting, or committing some heinous crime. In most cases, the criminal is tried and receives a prison term.

Not so with organized and corporate criminals. They have criminally woven together organized and corporate crime so seamlessly that it is difficult to uncover and prosecute. Today's super thefts are right inside all avenues of society, politics, and corporate entities.

The mafia, who used to traffic alcohol and drugs and were involved in gambling, prostitution, and other forms of illegal activity, have found a new and rather safe haven to make and launder money, areas such as politics, corporations, and even retirement villages

Once inside a given corporation or other mode of business, they power play their people into financial and executive positions. Their motive is profits, profits, and more profits—all at the expense of their suppliers and end users.

In order for organized crime to exist, it is necessary to corrupt the respected members of targeted organizations via bribery, sex, blackmail, or other forms of enticement. Even judicial and police officers are targeted for control by the mafia.

Today, organized crime has entered into Internet commerce, which discourages consumers from using the Internet for e-commerce.

Organized crime syndicates have gone global to work in cooperation with each other, and their corrupt tentacles stretch throughout the world.

Just as racket-ridden as the organized crime are the corrupt criminal lawyers, who use every legal ploy to release arrested offenders and avoid prosecution.

Today's super thefts are right inside all avenues of society, politics and corporate entities.

There is no way to stamp out organized and corporate crime entirely, any more than you can completely snuff out all the crabgrass in your lawn.

It is amazing, however, how the Lord God utilizes such criminal organizations to propagate and advance the livelihood of His people. This does not, in any way, condone the unrighteous behavior of the criminal element. It just shows how Almighty God can use even the bad to promulgate the good.

Time is truly drawing nigh, however, for the Lord's return is imminent, during which He will set up His theological kingdom and separate the wheat from the chaff.

My commission is to warn all, regardless of their sinful past life, to repent and ask the Lord for forgiveness. We all have fallen short of the glory of God. Salvation comes to those who realize their unrighteousness and willfully turn from the darkness of evil into the light of goodness.

Regardless where you are or what you have done, you can still receive pardon from the Lord. Did He not tell one of the criminals on the cross, "You will be with me in heaven?" Fear not any retaliation when reaching out for Christ's salvation, for the Lord is your safeguard. He will protect you.

Proverbs 4:19 The path of the wicked is like darkness, for they know not of what they stumble.

Proverbs 4:18 The path of the just is like the shining light that shines more and more until that perfect day.

(50)
Is Gambling a Sin, an Unprofitable Waste of Time, or Both?

DOES ONE LABEL GAMBLING A sin, a crime, a vice, or just an unprofitable waste of time? While it might be just a lottery ticket, a small bet at the racetrack, a few quarters in the slot machine, or a couple dollars at the blackjack card table, people in general say, "Oh, it's just an innocent pastime."

And the anecdote by some is, "I'll give some of the winnings to the church or some other worthy cause." It may behoove you to know that very few donate any of their newly won monies. Worse yet, the vast majority of the people who win are in worse financial shape a few years after winning than they were before.

Proverbs 13:11 states, "Dishonest money dwindles away, but he who gathers money little by little makes it grow."

While the Bible does not specifically condemn gambling or the lottery, the scriptures tell us to stay away from get rich quick tactics.

Gambling, especially gambling too much, is not any different than drinking too much, eating too much, or purchasing worthless things. But that does not justify gambling.

On the economic side, there is no end product that results

from gambling. Sure, people are hired, but for what? Is it just a sure-fire way to legally steal people's money? In order to institute businesses that do hire people and provide an end product, some suggest that casinos, lotteries and other gambling institutions donate 5 percent of their profits to assure new business ventures. An executive board of an accountant, executive, marketing expert, and a banker could lend the money to start-up, end-product type businesses.

Right now, gambling institutions donate some monies to schools, senior citizens, and surrounding communities. While this is good and should be continued, you'd be surprised how much of that donated money ends up in the hands of crooked politicians and lawyers.

One of the real financial dangers to those who play the slots, dice, or cards at the casino are the free—or even the paid—alcoholic beverages. Drinking can greatly alter a player's good reasoning to the point of losing a small, and sometimes a large, fortune.

Some may say, "Well, did not the apostles cast lots to see who would replace Judas?" The casting lots there, as in others instances in the Bible, was the eventual decision of the Lord God, not man.

Many wealthy and famous people find themselves surrounded by admiring onlookers and, coupled with too much drinking, they, too, lose large fortunes. So, the rich as well as the poor succumb to the addictive and mind-controlling allure of gambling. It is sad but true that it is the lower class who, for the most part, buy the lottery ticket, and they can least afford it.

Gambling casinos and lotteries are popping up in the majority of the states, cities, and counties, which will provide easy access to all.

The Lord states in I Timothy, "For the love of money is the root of all kinds of evil." It is no secret that gambling can lead to addiction, financial ruin, corruption, bad judgment, covetousness, waste of productive time, and a host of other unrighteous behaviors. All of these are coupled with the motivation of greed by both the house as well as the gambler.

Catholics consider gambling (since they do have bingo nights) to be okay as long as it is honest, with moderate stakes, within the financial measure of the players, and is played with the player's own money.

Protestants believe that gambling violates good work ethics and prudence. They also believe it is not within God's precepts in that it encourages greed.

While gambling may not be a spiritual ticket to hell, many have found that their losses have made their life here on earth a living hell.

In perspective, many say that the largest gambling arena in the world is the stock market. People there are betting that a given company will increase its market share, profitability, and pocketbook.

One can guess the pertinent question is, has anyone ever instituted a casino with the burning desire to help mankind? Or is it, again, just a sure-fire way of rigging a situation where you simply cannot lose but provide a seemingly wholesome way for people to recreationally lose money. Gambling casinos use mathematical algorithms in their gambling software to ensure that only a small amount of total intake dollars is taken from their coffers.

Gambling casinos generate more revenue than Hollywood movies, music, and video games combined. And now they have spread their alleged game of chance onto the Internet.

A 2002 report shows that between 10 percent and 17 percent of teenagers have a gambling problem because of their participation in internet gambling.

From an economic standpoint, for every dollar generated by gambling, the government spends ten dollars fighting it in areas of prostitution, embezzlement, bad checks, police corruption, and a host of other social problems.

Another report shows that one in five problem gamblers commit suicide. In fact, the suicide rate among gamblers is 150 percent higher than the norm.

The moot question here is --- does the end result of gambling justify the means?

Can you not see where hanging around gambling areas is not a healthy place to be? Many feel that it is demonically based and is the primary way one can become possessed into financial ruin.

Pavlov's theory is best exemplified with the slot's tingling sound of a winning jackpot that begins the never-ending saga of an addictive player trying again and again to get that ding-ding-ding-ding-ding rush.

Proverbs 23:5 For ungainly riches certainly make themselves wings and fly away like and eagle.

(51)

Taking Down the Ten Commandments

Secular, agnostic, and atheistic minority groups' viewpoints have willfully blinded the Congress and judicial system. Throughout America and other parts of the world, huge cranes hoist away stone tables bearing the Ten Commandments. Our government and judicial system are hell-bent on satisfying the wants and desires of sometimes only one person, while totally dismissing the spiritual inheritance of hundreds of thousands, even hundreds of millions of people.

The Lord God gave us the Ten Commandments as a rule of thumb for everyday living. The Ten Commandments are the cornerstone for almost all law throughout the world. They keep people on the right side of the spiritual road so to speak.

The Lord God, in His supreme wisdom, knew that Satan could cause all (yes, I mean all of us) to break those commandments, leading us into the very pits of Hades. In His love for mankind, the Lord God gave us grace (unmerited favor). That grace is Jesus Christ, the only begotten Son of the Living God. And whosoever accepts Jesus as their Lord and Savior shall have eternal life.

But the Ten Commandments is a visible word of God, in that we know when we have transgressed His laws. How can future generations repent if they do not know the laws they trespassed?

Our government and judicial system think that the secular minority groups will be satisfied by taking down the Ten Commandments only in public arenas. But they are sadly mistaken, as such minority groups will never be satisfied until they completely obliterate the Word of God.

For you see, such Godless groups, as well as select members of government and the judicial system, are not even of the seed of God. They have ears that do not hear and eyes that do not see God's Word. They then willfully become the seed of Satan.

Such political and judicial leaders make a straight line crooked, and their plumb line is off center. So, how can they possibly stay within the precepts of Almighty God?

Yet, these people have been put into governmental, educational, judicial, and other important decision-making positions in society.

Your prayers can change all this. You can start a prayer revolution that does not involve any physical activity at all. That is how strong prayer by the Lord's people is acted on by Almighty God.

Begin this very day to pray that the Lord God opens the eyes and ears of important decision-making people, so they realize how far off base they are in adhering to God's Word. Then, sit back and watch the angels of God root out all demonic evil in high positions.

Yes, the Lord God is at work!

Proverbs 15:3, 8 The eyes of the Lord are in every place, beholding the evil and the good. The sacrifice of the wicked is an abomination to the Lord … but the prayer of the upright is His delight and will not go unrewarded.

(52)
Not Honoring a Sabbath Day

THE NATIONS OF THE WORLD are on a fast lane approaching a 24/7 week. To paraphrase *Alice in Wonderland*'s Mad Hatter, "No time to rest. I'm late. I'm late for a very important date. Can't even say hello, good-bye, I'm late. I'm late. I'm late!"

Be it Sunday, Saturday, Friday, or any other day of the week, we should devote time to pay homage to the Lord God in respect of all He does for us.

* The Lord Jesus tells us not to make any one day more special than any other day, as all days are of His making. But as a nation, Christians have historically devoted Sunday to an official day of rest. To the Jews it is Saturday. To the Muslims it is Friday. And it is other days for other religious sects.

   What should we do and not do on a day of sacred rest?

* First and foremost is to set aside time (by yourself) for prayer.
* Attend a church or assembly where you pray and fellowship together, for it is the group prayers that hold down the evil power and principalities.
* Fast somewhat in that you do not intake as much food as usual, for it is a time to feed your spirit and soul, not your flesh.

* Refrain from any foul language and especially do not use the Lord's name in vain, for the day will not end before you are punished.
* Abstain from any form of alcohol or drugs that can alter your mind.
* At home, raise your hands and orally give praise to the Lord for all that you have … and then tell Him out loud of all your problem areas, and give Him thanks and praise for the manner and way He will take care of them.
* Carry on a conversation with the family members. Give each time to convey her thoughts and emotions of what she cares about and intends to accomplish.
* Sit back and quietly (by yourself) for at least a half hour and reflect on your life and where you are going.
* Conclude by again thanking the Lord for not only listening to your prayers and requests but for also taking care of the them.

Some people attend church any day of the week, not just on Sunday. They donate their financial share, and especially respect Sunday as other religions respect their sacred day. However, they find more solitude and relaxation during the less crowded weekday at church and can concentrate more effectively. But that is your own choice.

It is important do know this much: not having Sunday as a day of rest is putting too much emotional stress on the nation and its people.

Have you noticed that Chick-fil-A (a very successful restaurant) is not open on Sunday? Personally, I feel a certain kind of guilt on entering a bank or some other commercial institution on Sunday. Occasionally I do it, but I can tell you it is not without some sort of condemnatory cloud hanging over my head.

We are no different than others in finding ourselves amid people running to and fro in department stores, banks, ballparks, fast-food restaurants, or endless Little League ball games.

Maybe we just all need to spend one day with the Lord, as life as we now know it is just too demanding with all the accidents, wars, and social unrest. Maybe we need to take one day out of the seven-day week and somehow take some time to thank the Lord God for His blessings.

Hospitals and doctors are always on call almost 24/7 at times. So, life as we once knew it is on a faster pace due to increased population and a host of other things that coincide with it.

But let's not forget who made us.

If we as a nation had to work seven days a week, like the Egyptians made the Jews do to make the ancient pyramids, we would be so grateful to rest and worship one day a week. Or, if we lived in a country where the Christians are under deadly slaughter by terrorists, we again would so dearly appreciated the opportunity to worship in group fellowship.

As the old saying goes, "We never appreciate something until we no longer have it." We should never take for granted the blessings the Lord God bestows on us. Remember, it is our group prayers and praise in the church that asks God to hold down the evil powers and principalities.

The most important inheritance you can give to your children is the knowledge of the blessings the Lord bestows on those who worship and set aside one day a week especially for Him.

America is a Christian nation with the day of Sunday as its official day-of-rest offering unto the Lord God. I feel that any person, company, nation, or other form of institution who rest and give praise to God on that day will receive His blessings.

Psalm 95:3–6 For the Lord is a great God, and a great King above all gods. Come and let us kneel before the Lord our maker.

(53)
Betrayal

BETRAYAL IS AS OLD AS life itself. You read about it when Satan betrayed Eve and eventually Adam in the Garden of Eden.

There is not a person alive or dead who has not in some way or another been betrayed. It's how you handle it that counts. You can go ballistic, foolish, shamed … or you can rise up to the jilted situation and say, "If the Lord be with me then who can be against me?"

If you think you have never been betrayed, you are living with your head in the sand. This does not mean you go around looking for evidence of betrayal. It just means it is as prevalent as the air you breathe. Rain also occurs, but you do not go looking for rain all the time. It just means you must be prepared in case it does occur. And being prepared means staying tucked in the word of God.

Think about it.

Was not even the Lord of Lords, Jesus Christ, betrayed? Just ask Judas. And were not all the martyrs, prophets, apostles, and saints somehow betrayed? Yep, they all felt the almost paralyzing sting of betrayal. And did not Satan betray one-third of all the angels who were cast out of heaven with him?

Now I ask you: Who is the most paranoid, egomaniac, self-serving individual that ever treaded on earth?

The answer is—Satan!

Now, if Satan knows that all the saints, martyrs, prophets, apostles, and some angels were betrayed, and even the Lord Jesus Christ was betrayed, do you not think he is immeasurably concerned about the same thing happening to him?

So, how can Satan prevent anyone from betraying him?

Since he does not have the ability to know what's in the deep recesses of the human mind and heart (as does the Lord God), he is trying to derive that information electronically, via computer "black psychology." As explained earlier, the human mind is basically digital and analog. Satan will try to determine electronically whether a person is lying or telling the truth.

But more than that, Satan reads and studies the Bible forward and backward. He knows that if anyone receives the infamous Satanic 666 on his person, he cannot enter heaven.

So Satan, in his attempt to stop any form of betrayal, will insist that all must have the 666 inserted on their person, preferably on their forehead or right hand. And all who do not have this 666 mark will be immediately assassinated.

Do you want to be around when Satan is in control? Do you want to be taken up by the Lord Jesus Christ's rapture before the end-time tribulation? Do you want to get out of the darkness in which you find yourself and get into the light of Jesus Christ?

Then say this prayer:

Father God, I accept Your only begotten Son, Jesus Christ as my Lord and Savior. I truly ask for your forgiveness of all my sins and unrighteousness. And I deeply request that your Holy Spirit enters me so that I can be raised up at the end times when my Lord and Savior, Jesus Christ, returns and raptures His brothers and sisters into Heaven.

From here, you should attend a born-again church; have fellowship with the brothers and sisters of the Lord; give financially to your church, the poor, and the less fortunate; read the scriptures (at least a page a day); and pray in all that you do—including your work, family, eating, and what you plan to do; abstain from all forms of swearing; read and view only that which is wholesome; and ask the Lord's angels to look after you and your family.

The end time is basically a seven-year period. The rapture will come before this satanic period. And the only way a person can get to heaven during that seven-year period is by not accepting the 666 mark of the beast and by receiving a martyr's death.

Revelation 20:10 And the devil was cast into the lake of fire and brimstone where the beast and false prophet are and tormented day and night forever.

Revelation 20:11–14 And a great White Throne where sat Father God and Jesus with the Book of Life. And all that were dead from the ground, sea and Hades were raised up and stood before God where they were judged according to their works. And whoever was not found in the Book of Life was cast into the lake of fire and brimstone.

Believe me, all this is true! You want to be found in that Book of Life!

(54)
Asteroid Impact

LARGE ASTEROIDS IMPACT MOTHER EARTH about every one thousand years. And we are about due for another one. Meteors also impact earth (once they hit earth, they are called meteorites), but they are thousands to millions of tons smaller than an asteroid.

Asteroids hurtle through space at more than forty thousand miles per hour. An asteroid one-half mile in diameter, impacting the earth in the Atlantic Ocean, would cause tremendous devastation to the earth's environment and human life as we know it.

Eons ago, the six-mile-wide asteroid that formed the 110-mile-wide crater in the Gulf of Mexico was part of a group of asteroids that smashed into the earth. It changed the earth so radically that many scientists conclude that it terminated the dinosaurs that roamed the earth. And the asteroid in 1994 that hit the planet Juniper had a force larger than all the nuclear bombs in the world, and two planets the size of earth could fit side by side in the crater it formed.

If a half-mile wide asteroid hit the Atlantic Ocean, you could expect: (1) three hundred- to five hundred-foot high tidal waves that would wipe out Florida, New Orleans, New York, New Jersey, and other coastal cities throughout the world. (2) Thousands of sunken ships would cause international trade to come to a complete halt. (3) Weather patterns would become so severe that many would be flooded, even in the inland areas, while others would wither in exhausting heat. (4) Gigantic hurricanes, tornadoes, earthquakes, and torrential electrical storms would occur. (5) There would be tremendous loss of sea life and drinking water would be contaminated. These are just a few of the devastating nightmares that would plague the world.

Please note that in September 2007, an asteroid crashed into southern Peru, leaving a crater fifteen feet deep and sixty-five feet wide. Is this the beginning of something?

Mankind is powerless when it comes to stopping or altering the course of an asteroid. Even if they blasted it apart, the plummeting remains of the asteroid would cause equal if not more devastation on earth.

An asteroid about the size of a small truck and weighing around ten tons struck Canada in November 2008. Had it hit a downtown area, it would have devastated a good portion of it. And that was a rather small asteroid. Most asteroids travel at a speed of fifty thousand miles per hour in which the atmospheric pressure burns them up before hitting the ground. Since the Canadian asteroid traveled at a lesser speed, it was able to reach the earth somewhat intact.

On looking up the word "asteroid," you will find that they range in diameter from one to several hundred miles and orbit chiefly between Mars and Jupiter If you think that End Time asteroids are a figment of man's imagination and have not been prophesied, then look in the Book of Revelation where you will find the 7 seals, the 7 trumpets and the 7 bowls of wrath have been predicted over 2,000 years ago.

In the Book of Revelation 8: 8, you read where a great mountain burning with fire was cast into the sea and a third part of the sea creatures died and a third of the ships sunk. And in Revelation 8:9, you read where a great star called the Wormwood Star fell from the heavens and a great many men died because the drinking water was contaminated.

The tremendous size of some asteroids puts them in the category of minor planets or planetoids. There are over one hundred thousand such asteroids orbiting between Jupiter and Mars. The gravitational pull of Jupiter and Mars (some scientists consider it is air pressure, not gravity) keeps the asteroids from pulling free from their orbit. However, due to some anomaly, an asteroid can break free from its gravitational pull to roam freely in the universe until it hits another planet or some other celestial body..

In Revelation 8:8, you read where a great mountain burning with fire was cast into the sea, and a third of the sea creatures died and a third of the ships sunk. And in Revelation 8:9, you read where a great star called the Wormwood Star fell from the heavens, and a great many men died because the drinking water was contaminated. Personally, I wonder about the Wormwood Star, as my ancestor's former last name was Wormwood (Joseph Warren Wormwood, 1881–1919).

Psalm 114:7 Tremble the earth at the presence of the Lord.

Psalm 18:13 The Lord thundered in the heaven bringing forth coals of fire.

(55)
Tick-Tock ... the Doomsday Atomic Clock

AN ATOMIC CLOCK IS A time-keeping device controlled by atomic or molecular oscillation, as opposed to a mechanical clock or watch that uses oscillating balance wheels, pendulums, and tuning forks.

The first atomic clock was invented in 1948, using the vibration of ammonia molecules. Today's atomic clocks cannot lose or gain a second in twenty million years.

Much of our life and how we live is built around the atomic clock. The atomic clock is used for the GPS automobile and sea navigation systems, for the precise carrier frequency for radio stations, for wireless alarm clocks, for satellite navigation systems, for tracking space vehicles, as well as many other technological uses.

The *Bulletin of Atomic Scientists, (BAS)*, analyzes the world's survival chances from world political, environmental, and technological developments. The board of directors of the *BAS* maintains the Doomsday Clock, a clock face that indicates when a combination of earthly abnormal conditions will completely annihilate the world as we presently know it, pushing the Doomsday Clock to strike midnight.

Presently, the Doomsday Clock reads 11:55 PM. So, we have precariously and potentially lived over 98 percent of our existence, as we now know it, because of some of the following reasons:

- Nuclear weapons can be launched at a moment's notice.
- Pakistan and India are at a nuclear standoff.
- North Korea and other smaller nations now have access to nuclear weapons.
- Nuclear power plants across the world have made the sale and possession of nuclear materials easily accessible by terrorist groups.
- Global warming is a global threat, but it is slightly less of one than a terrorist nuclear holocaust.
- Nanotechnology and genetic engineering may perform precise surgery, but it also makes it possible to make a dirty bomb to fit inside a small briefcase.
- Wars are erupting throughout the globe, and terrorists groups are spreading across the world.
- Severe weather outbreaks have increased, along with volcanoes, earthquakes, and tsunamis.
- The United States and Russia currently have more than twenty-six thousand nuclear weapons.
- Population has grown exponentially to the point of not possibly not producing enough food for world survival.
- Global oil reserves have peaked, with no world backup energy system in place.
- There is no real answer for how to avoid asteroid catastrophe.
- The morality of the world (as evidenced by many of the unrighteous areas listed in this book) is

at its lowest level and lends itself to a spiritual Sodom and Gomorrah holocaust.

Note: * The Doomsday Clock does not include spiritual immorality in its calculations, but you can easily see where it does play the most significant part.

Note: World prayer and repentance can hold back all the above world tragedies.

Psalm 9:9 The Lord God is a refuge for the oppressed in times of trouble.

(56)
Almighty God's Morality Atomic Clock

As you saw before, man's Doomsday Clock spells out the various world events that signify the end time is near, due to the vast number of atomic weapons, wars and various other hostilities, and environmental problems in the world.

On the other hand, Almighty God's Morality Atomic Clock is also clicking away, and the time is drawing nigh. You have heard this end-time warning time and time again. And I can tell you this: it was because people renewed their ways and became more righteous that the Lord God held back the final judgment.

Right this moment, due to so much immoral and unrighteous on earth, time is truly drawing nigh. Unless we change our spiritual outlook and see and hear the words of God, there is little chance of halting this final deity decree.

The world is more than ever filled with abortions, homosexuality, racketeering, gambling, hedonistic pleasures, political intrigue, lawlessness, malfeasant judges and attorneys, homeless children, foul entertainment, adultery, idolatry, fornication, lying, stealing, cheating, embezzlement, bribes, murder, wicked gossip, depraved demonic possession, sloth, greed, and a host of other ungodly ways of thinking, speaking, and living.

Father God gave unto us the grace and mercy of His only

begotten Son, Jesus Christ. We are to try to follow the Ten Commandments, and when and where we fail or fall short, we are to sense our shortcomings and ask Christ to go to the Father and petition for our forgiveness.

But the people basically feel that they can live their own life the way they want to live without any earthly or spiritual consequences.

Believe me, such is not the case.

The protective umbrella of grace and mercy provided by Jesus Christ is the only way to receive protection on earth as well as forgiveness and eternal salvation.

If you could only see the unfathomable, glorious, magnificent, and enraptured allure of heavenly beings and the various levels of heaven, leading to the judgment seat of the Lord God, clothed with shining white robe, with His head of hair white like wool, and His eyes like a flame of fire. Shooting from His mouth is a sharp two-edged sword, saying, "I am the Alpha and the Omega, the beginning and the end. I am He that lived, and was dead, and behold, I am alive for evermore. Amen, and have the keys to Hades and of the dead."

Around the throne is a rainbow, and twenty-four elders fall down before the Lord Jesus and cast their golden crowns before Him, for no one was worthy to open the end-time seals. One of the elders said, "Weep not as the Lion of the tribe of Judah, the root of David has prevailed and is the only one worthy to open the end-time seals."

The end-time seals have been prophesied many times over the centuries. While many mocked the prophets, those who turned from their sinful ways are the very ones who suspended the predicted judgment.

Remember also that one thousand years of man's time on earth is but one day to the Lord in heaven. While you think the judgment is but a figment of prophetic imagination, you yourself may soon pass away, for your life on this earth is but a blade of grass ready to be stepped on.

It behooves us to remember that, if you do pass away before the end-time judgment, you surely will want to be taken out of your grave and ascend heaven when the end-time seals are opened and the angel's trumpets signify the rapture of Jesus' people.

As you stand before the Lord, written down in the Book of Life will be all the things that you thought, said, and did (both good and bad).

You will gulp in your thoughts of whether the angels of good will sweep you into heaven or if the angels of evil will whisk you into the fires of hell. The truth of this brings tears to my eyes of the glorious moment for those who are found worthy to enter the kingdom of heaven. My heart sinks so low for those who are not found righteously commendable and are swept away thrashing, weeping, and gnashing their teeth as they are tossed outside the gates of heaven into the fiery pit of hell.

For you who choose not to believe in the end-time judgment of God, who mock His past and present warnings, my prayerful petition of this book is to bring you out of the devil's darkness and into the Light of Jesus Christ.

Truly, time is drawing nigh. You may not see or live the final end-time judgment when the seals are opened and the angel's trumpets herald the coming of the Lord Jesus with His unfathomable gathering of angels, but your soul in the grave will know and burst forth with delight or doom. It all depends on you. You alone, regardless of your past, can now ask the Lord for forgiveness and the gift of His Holy Spirit to be raised up from the dead on His returning rapture.

Almighty God's Morality Atomic Clock is drawing toward midnight. Time is drawing nigh. Get yourself Jesus' rapture ready. Yes indeed, Jesus is coming soon!

Psalm 7:8–9 The Lord shall judge the peoples, and the wickedness of the wicked shall come to an end.

Luke 13:3 Jesus said, "Unless you repent, you shall perish."

The Big Reason Time Is Drawing Nigh: The Antichrist

THE LORD GOD IS SOVEREIGN. He is omnipotent (all powerful). He is omniscient (all knowing). He is omnipresent (present everywhere). He is omnificent (all creative). He is the everlasting God who lives in the present, past, and future all at one time.

He, however, allows His people to live freely and independently of His control unless they ask for divine help.

The devil on earth and in the atmosphere also has tremendous spiritual and physical capabilities. As great as they are, the devil and all his fallen angels are beneath and less in greatness of the Lord God—even though Satan believes he is greater and more justified in his evil endeavors and arrogant pride.

Evil has its beginning whenever one falls away from the Word of God. And the very beginning of evil for mankind was when the devil made Adam and Eve disobey God's Word.

"Anti" means "opposite." The name Antichrist means the opposite of the Lord God. And Satan's angels strive to impart their evil (opposite of God's word) in the minds of the people on earth. The devil will do this until the time is ripe for his eventual takeover.

The question is: Is that time fast approaching, almost like—now? Who knows? Here are some of the reasons it may very well be.

A person who has the satanic capability to take over the following areas of society can rule the people on earth. He must infiltrate (1) the media (newspapers, radio, TV, computer, and other modes of mass communication); (2) the justice system (corrupt and unrighteous lawyers, judges, and police); (3) the banking system (money buys and corrupts); (4) the political arena (a monarchy where people will condone anyone who can bring peace from terrorist's threats and chaotic violence); (5) the religious system (for the people must believe that which is being done is moral and upright). Remember that the Lord God said, "At the end times even the very elect will be deceived." That is, unless He intervenes; (6) the food, water, and economic distribution system, for people will do almost anything to be employed and eat; (7) the military (to control the disbelievers militarily).

Can you not see that it only takes a minority (10 to 20 percent of the population) who ban together (under the spiritual control of Satan) to control all of the above areas of society?

Minority secular and atheistic organizations are hell-bent on controlling society. They are not of the seed of Almighty God but the disobedient seed of the Antichrist. They believe not in God's Word but in their own way of thinking and living.

Right now, the above-listed areas are being infiltrated and overtaken by bold and unchecked immoral, secular minorities who get their illegal ways by first infiltrating the justice system and then the media. Like dominoes, the rest of the controlling factors will fall in place.

Satan does all this by setting up his disobedient people of God's word in seemingly beneficial organizations who stealthily strive to change and destroy society's rules and regulations, like appearing to state legally that the Constitution is wrong in church vs. state regulations; condemning the showing of the Ten Commandments; banning school prayer; promoting the right of free (vulgar) speech and pornography; legalizing abortions (without the fetus receiving due process of law); instituting politically correct speech; congressionally outlawing one to speak out against immoral, secular minorities that legalize homosexual marriages; legalizing pedophiles in school and organized (Boy and Girl Scouts) organizations; and a host of other demonic, malicious inclusions in society to the point that the judicial system overrules and scares the government into submission to their demanding ways.

What makes all this possible is the computer. The electronic system is now in place for the Antichrist to make his physical appearance.

And terrorists will continue to carry out their threats and violent behavior until the people will do anything to caress peace.

Yes, the answer will be a well-received standing ovation by the world for one world government ruled by a person who can put down the arsenal of terrorist bombs. This person must be someone the Islamic terrorists believe is the leader for whom they have been waiting. They will bow down to him, and his miraculous capabilities will encourage other religions to also consider him to be the one who was sent to bring peace and prosperity.

This Antichrist will rule the earth for a three-and-one-half-year period of peace and prosperity. Jesus Christ will have already taken \his people from the earth, and the Holy Spirit will no longer be on the earth to hold down the evil and demonic powers and principalities.

And for the next three and one-half years, the real wicked ways of the Antichrist will appear. He will demand that those on earth can only work and eat if they have the 666 mark on their hand or forehead. Demonic activity will be so harsh that people's knees will knock with fear and their bowels will gush out from the hellish demands on them.

And the only way those left on earth can get to heaven is by martyrdom. They will be killed for not receiving the 666 mark on their hand or forehead.

The time is fast approaching for the Antichrist to take over. The world stage is set, and the opening curtain is ready to be pulled by Satan to introduce the Antichrist as the false peacekeeper.

The only thing that can keep that final curtain from opening is if the Lord's people change and strive to help others to repent and find the Lord. When Abraham begged the Lord to save Sodom and Gomorrah from destruction, the Lord said, "'I will save it if ten persons can be found righteous.'" But ten righteous persons could not be found.

When the Antichrist becomes ruler, there will not be one righteous person left on earth. All fall short of God's righteousness; it is through the acceptance of His only begotten Son, Jesus Christ, that one is saved and found righteous. So, those left on earth to the apocalyptic, prince of darkness, are the ones who failed to repent and did not believe in the salvation of God's only begotten Son, Jesus Christ.

When the final, end-time curtain opens, those who applaud the Antichrist are those who disobeyed God's Word (the word turned flesh in Christ), and their reward will be hell on earth and eternal damnation.

Please bear in mind, the intention in conveying all this is not to condemn the readers but to lead them to salvation out of this coming Judgment Day, for the Lord will detain everything if His people repent and return to righteous behavior.

And the key to opening the door to heaven and not being around during this coming wholesale destruction of life is to repent, to ask God for the forgiveness of your sins, to mend your ways, and to accept His only begotten Son, Jesus Christ, as your Lord and Savior.

Yes, it is as simple and true as that, for the definition of "grace" (Jesus) is "unmerited favor." No one deserves it. You simply ask for His mercy and divine intervention to save you, and it is your automatic rapture ticket for all eternity.

Matthew 16:23 So says the Lord, "Get thee behind me, Satan, you art an offense unto me; for you savor not the things that be of God, but those that be of men."

What Awaits Those Who Work for and Accept the Antichrist: Sorrow and Despair

Sorrow and Despair

AS WAS MENTIONED, THE FIRST three and one-half years of the Antichrist's reign will be utterly wonderful in the ears, eyes, and minds of the people. Peace and prosperity will flourish, and people will renounce the Christians who somehow disappeared as the very cause of their problems that existed before the Antichrist's arrival.

But, the next three and one-half years will make them devastatingly sorry to even be alive.

That is when the warped, vicious side of the Antichrist becomes evident, for Satan hates mankind. He despises all but himself. He is filled with pride, mistrust, and violent revenge.

Satan knows full well that even Jesus was betrayed, as well as all His various prophets before Him. Knowing this, Satan (who believes he is equal to God) will set up the Antichrist to equate to Jesus, the beast to equal the Holy Spirit and himself as God. Then, to make sure no one betrays him, Satan will introduce the infamous 666 mark.

And he will bring an onslaught of violence against all who do not accept his 666 mark. Without the 666 on either their hand or forehead, the people cannot buy or sell, or do anything for that matter. And they also know that once they commit to the 666, they have separated themselves from God and have condemned themselves to eternal damnation.

Fear, danger, unnerving apprehension, extreme dread, and stalking terror will follow them like their own shadow. People's knees will knock from fearful thoughts, and they will disembowel themselves in nervous alarm of even a knock on their door.

Then, an even more horrible fate awaits them: the end-time Apocalypse. That is when Almighty God's judgment is poured out on all those who do not believe in His Son's salvaging grace, God's only begotten son of mercy, Jesus Christ. Mankind cannot comprehend the horror of this end-time judgment.

Many ask how a God who is filled with love, mercy, and grace instill such a worldwide plague on mankind. The people left on earth after the seven-year period of the Antichrist are those filled with hate, murderous malignancy, and who are unmerciful in their treatment of others—so much so that they will even curse God during the apocalyptic tribulation period. And they will curse God even when they are cast into the fiery pits of hell.

God's judgment on them is in direct proportion to their judgment on His people. The followers of the Antichrist raped, maimed, tortured, and killed the Christians, and their tribulation punishment is the fitting reward for their hatred of God and His people.

But, it is wise to remember that even though a person commits all of the above sins before the tribulation period, he or she is saved if they truly repent, accept Jesus Christ as their Lord and Savior, and ask for the Holy Spirit of God to enter their mind, heart, and soul.

Revelation 22:14–15 Blessed are they who follow the Lord's commandments, for they have the right to the "Tree of Life" and may enter the new Jerusalem … but cast out are the whoremongers, murders, idolaters, and whosoever loves and makes lies.

THE BOOK OF REVELATION (ARMAGEDDON: PROPHECY OF THE END TIMES)

Worthy Is the Lamb to Open the End-Time Seals

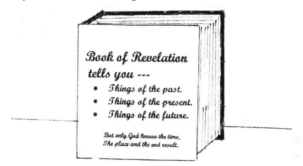

Book of Revelation tells you ---
- Things of the past.
- Things of the present.
- Things of the future.

But only God knows the time,
The place and the end result.

A THRONE STOOD IN HEAVEN, upon which God radiantly sat. Around the throne is a rainbow and twenty-four elders sit in white garments and with golden crowns on their heads that represent the twelve tribes of Israel and the twelve apostles of the Lamb.

From the throne comes flashes of lightning, peals of thunder, with seven lamps of fire that represent the seven spirits of God. And around the throne were four creatures. The first creature was like a lion, the second had a face like that of a calf, the third creature had a face like that of man, and the fourth creature like that of a flying eagle. Each creature had six wings, with eyes around and within. Day and night they sang, "Holy, holy, holy is the Lord God, the Almighty, who was and who is and who is to come."

And the Lord said, "I am the Alpha and the Omega, the beginning and the end." And the Lord spoke of the seven angels who represented the seven churches: Ephesus, Smyrna, Pergamos, Thyatira, Sardis, Philadelphia, and Laodicea. He spoke of the good and bad of each church of that time and the time to come.

And at the right hand of Him sat a book with seven seals, and an angel proclaimed, "Who is worthy to open the book and break the seals?"

No one was found worthy in heaven or on earth … except a Lamb, standing as if slain, with seven horns and seven eyes that are the seven spirits of the Lord. The Lamb took the book out of the hand of Him who sat on the throne, and the four living creatures and the twenty-four elders fell down before the Lamb and sang, "Worthy are You to take the book and open its seals, for You were slain and did purchase for God with Your blood."

The Seven End-Time Seals

The Seven End Time Seals

| White Horse Conquer 1. | Red Horse War 2. | Black Horse Famine 3. | Pale Horse Death 4. | Martyrs Revenge 5. | Earthquake Sun, Moon Stars fall. 6. | Trumpets Given to Angels 7. |

THE END-TIME APOCALYPSE BEGINS WITH the Lamb opening the seven end-time seals.

The first seal opened by the Lamb brings the sound of thundering hoofs of a white horse, its rider coming to conquer the people.

The second seal opened by the Lamb is the red horse, whose rider comes to wage wars.

The third seal opened by the Lamb is a black horse, whose rider has a balance in his hand to bring famine to the land.

The fourth seal opened by the Lamb is a pale horse, whose rider, named Death, brings pestilence, disease, and loss of life.

The fifth seal opened by the Lamb exposes the souls of saints who were martyred for witnessing the Word of God.

They were given a white robe and told to wait until their number was complete.

The sixth seal opened by the Lamb is a great earthquake, which turned the sun black, the moon like blood, stars fell from the sky, mountains and islands disappeared, and the murderous people of the earth hid from the wrath of God.

Then, four angels held back the winds of the four corners of the earth so that one hundred forty-four thousand Israelites (twelve thousand from each of the twelve tribes of Israel) and a great multitude from other nations of the earth who came out of the great tribulation with their robes washed clean from the blood of the Lamb, Jesus Christ, could come forth.

Then the Lamb opened the seventh seal, and the seven angels who stood before God were given trumpets.

The Seven End-Time Trumpets

1. Hail, fire and blood destroyed 1/3 of the earth.
2. Mountain of fire tossed into the sea destroys 1/3 of ships & life.
3. Wormwood star falls from sky and destroys drinking water.
4. One third of the sun, moon and stars blacken.
5. Key to bottomless pit releases scorpion like locusts.
6. Four angels Freed from Euphrates River Kill 1/3 of Mankind. Two prophets.
7. Kingdom of the World is now The Kingdom of God. 144,000 Israelites

THE FIRST ANGEL BLEW THE first trumpet, and hail and fire mixed with blood fell on the earth and burned a third of it.

The second angel blew the second trumpet, and a great mountain, burning with fire, was tossed into the sea of blood, and a third of all the creatures and ships were destroyed.

The third angel blew the third trumpet and a great star called Wormwood fell blazing from heaven and made bitter a third of all the rivers and fountains, which caused many to die.

The fourth angel blew the fourth trumpet and a third part the sun, moon, and stars were darkened; a third of day and night were kept from shining.

The fifth angel blew the fifth trumpet, and a star fell from the sky. The angel was then given a key to open the bottomless pit, from which came smoke. And out of the smoke came locusts, looking like horses arrayed for battle. The locusts had gold crowns on their heads, faces like a human, hair like a woman, teeth like a lion, scales like iron breastplates, and wings that made noise like chariots charging into battle.

The locusts were led by Abaddon-Apollyon (Satan). They had tails like scorpions. Their sting lasted for five months, and the pain made men long to die rather than endure the pain. The locusts were told not to harm anything green or those with the seal of God on their foreheads.

The sixth angel blew the sixth trumpet, and a voice released the four angels who were bound at the Euphrates River. They released two hundred thousand cavalry troops, whose riders wore breastplates of the color of fire, sulfur, and sapphire. The heads of the horses were like those of lions, with fire, smoke, and sulfur shooting from their mouths, which killed a third of mankind.

Still, the rest of mankind did not repent or give up their sinful ways. Then another angel came with a scroll in his hand and set his right foot on the sea and his left foot on land.

A voice came from heaven and said not to write what was on the scroll, but a decree was issued that when the seventh trumpet was blown, the mystery of God shall be revealed. The angels told that the Holy City would be trampled for forty-two months, and two witnesses would have the power to prophesy for the forty-two months (1,260 days).

Two prophets of God had the power to stop the rain, turn water into blood, and smite the earth with every plague. The beast from the bottomless pit waged war with them and killed the two. They lay dead in the street for three and one-half days, while the people of the Antichrist rejoiced at their death.

Then the Lord breathed life back into them, and they rose in a cloud into heaven. The sinful people who rejoiced at their death became exceedingly fearful, as the earth quaked and seven thousand of them were killed. The rest began giving glory to God in heaven. The whole world shall see and witness the death and resurrection of the two prophets.

The seventh angel blew the seventh trumpet, and loud voices in heaven were heard saying, "The kingdom of the world has become the kingdom of the Lord and His Christ; and He will reign forever and ever."

And the temple of God was opened, and there appeared the Ark of the Covenant, accompanied by lightning, voices, an earthquake, and great hail.

Then appeared a woman clothed with the sun, the moon

under her feet, and on her head, was a crown of twelve stars; she was in pain with child. There also appeared a great red dragon with seven heads, ten horns, and seven crowns on his head. His tail swept a third of the stars from heaven to earth. The dragon stood, ready to devour the child at birth.

The woman had a male child who, was born to rule all nations. To flee the devil, she hid in the wilderness for 1,260 days. A war in heaven between Michael and his angels fought against the dragon, and he was thrown out of heaven down to the earth. A voice said, "Now the salvation, the power and the kingdom of God, and the authority of His Christ have come, for the blood of the Lamb has overcome the evil one."

Woe unto the earth, because the devil has come down unto you, having great wrath, as he knows he has only a short time. The devil pursued the woman to slay the child, and he poured water from his mouth like a river to drown the woman, but the earth opened its mouth and swallowed the river.

The dragon tried to wage war against the rest of the woman's offspring (those who were born again) and kept the Word of God to bear witness to Jesus. Then, out of the sea came a beast with seven heads, ten horns, and ten diadems on its horns. It was like a leopard with bear's feet and a lion's mouth. It received its power and authority from the dragon (Satan).

One of the beast's heads had a mortal wound, which was healed. The beast was given power and authority for forty-two months. Then, another beast rose out of the earth, and it had two horns like a lamb and spoke like the dragon. It made the people worship the first beast with ten horns. It worked great signs, such as making fire come down from heaven, and it killed the people who would not worship the first beast. It made everyone put the number 666 on their hand or forehead in order to buy or sell. Without the number, they cold do nothing to live.

Then, standing on Mount Zion, were the one hundred forty-four thousand Israelites who had the name of the Almighty God and Jesus on their foreheads. They were singing a song before the throne of God. Another angel was flying in mid-heaven, saying, "Fear God and give Him glory, because the hour of His judgment has come."

A second angel followed, saying, "Fallen, fallen is Babylon

who has made the nations drink the wine of passion of her immortality."

A third angel followed, saying, "If anyone worships the beast and his image and receives the 666 mark on his forehead or upon his hand, he will also drink the wrath of God … and he will be tormented with fire and brimstone in the presence of the holy angels and of the Lamb (Jesus). Their torment goes on forever."

Then came the call of the saints who kept the commandments of God and the faith of Jesus. The voice said, "Blessed are the dead who die in the Lord from now on."

Then, one like the son of man came out of the temple of heaven with a sharp sickle (like the Son of man), and an angel said, "Put in your sickle and reap, because the hour to reap has come, and the harvest of the earth is ripe."

Another angel came out to gather the vintage and threw it into the great winepress, and the blood flowed as high as a horse's bridle and for two hundred miles long.

The harvest of the first angel was for the saved in the faith of Jesus, and the harvest of the second angel was for the lost or wicked or those who disobeyed the Word of God who repented not nor accepted Almighty God's only begotten Son, Christ Jesus, as their Lord and Savior.

The Seven Bowls of Wrath

THEN SEVEN ANGELS CLOTHED IN pure white linen, their breasts girded with a golden band, were given seven bowls of wrath by one of the living creatures who served the Lord God.

The first angel poured the first bowl of wrath on the earth, and foul and evil sours came upon the people who bore the 666 mark of the beast and worshipped his image.

The second angel poured the second bowl of wrath into the sea, and it became like the blood of a dead man; every living thing in the sea died.

The third angel poured the third bowl of wrath into the rivers and into the fountains, and they became filled with blood. Then the angel of water praised the Lord, because the evil ones who had shed the blood of the saints and prophets now had blood as their drink.

The fourth angel poured the fourth bowl of wrath over the sun, and it scorched the sinful people with fire and fierce heat. Still, the unrighteous cursed God and did not repent of their immoral deeds.

The fifth angel poured the fifth bowl of wrath on the throne of the beast, and its kingdom was in darkness. Still, the sinful cursed God and did not repent of their sinful deeds.

The sixth angel poured the sixth bowl of wrath into the great river Euphrates, and its waters dried up. There was then issued from the mouth of the dragon, the beast, and the false prophet three foul spirits like frogs. They were demon spirits, sent to go abroad to the kings of the whole earth to assemble them for battle at Armageddon.

The seventh angel poured the seventh bowl of wrath into the air, and a voice from the temple said, "It is done!"

There was lightning, thunder, and an earthquake such as the world has never seen. Mountains and islands disappeared, cities fell, and there were hailstones as heavy as one hundred pounds. Still, the sinful cursed God and would not repent of their deeds.

After these things, another angel came from heaven. This angel had great authority, and the earth illuminated with his glory. He cried out, "Fallen, fallen is Babylon, the dwelling place of demons, she has committed acts of immorality and pestilence, mourning and famine will plague her and she will burn up with fire."

Then, a great multitude of voices in heaven were heard saying, "Hallelujah! Salvation and glory and power belong to our God, because his judgments are true and righteous."

Jesus, the Very Word of God

AFTER THIS, A MAN CALLED Faithful and True sitting on a white horse who in righteousness wages war. His eyes are like a flame of fire, and on His head are many crowns. He is clothed in a robe dipped in blood and His name is --- THE WORD OF GOD!

His armies are arrayed in white linen and mounted on white horses. On his robe is inscribed, KING OF KINGS and LORD OF LORDS.

And the kings of the earth, along with the beasts, gathered together to make war against the Lord God. And He took the beast, the false prophet, and those who worshipped the beast into the lake of burning fire.

An angel calls all the birds together to eat the flesh of those to be slaughtered. The beast and the false prophet are captured and thrown alive into the lake of fire that burns with brimstone.

Satan Thrown into the Pit of Fire and Brimstone

THEN AN ANGEL COMES DOWN from heaven with the key to the bottomless pit. He seizes the ancient serpent, the devil, and bounds him for one thousand years in the bottomless pit. After which, he will be loosed for a little season.

After the thousand years in prison, Satan gathers together the nations he deceived and brings them into battle against the beloved city. The devil and his army are defeated, and he is cast into the lake of fire, which already holds the beast and false prophet.

Then, those who have not worshipped the beast came to life to live with Christ for the one thousand years. The rest of the dead do not come to life until the one thousand years end. This is the first resurrection.

The Great White Throne

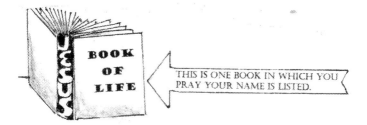

BOOK OF LIFE

THIS IS ONE BOOK IN WHICH YOU PRAY YOUR NAME IS LISTED.

THEN, A GREAT WHITE THRONE is seen, and He who sat upon it. All the dead stood before the throne, and the Book of Life is opened. The dead are judged by what is written in the book, by what they had done.

The sea, death, and Hades give up their dead to be judged.

Death, Hades, and all who are not written in the Book of Life are thrown into the lake of fire.

A New Heaven and a New Earth

THE NEW JERUSALEM COMES DOWN from heaven. A voice said, "God will be with mankind, and He will wipe away every tear and death would be no more." And He who sat on the throne says, "Behold I am making all things new … and he who overcomes shall inherit these things, and I will be His God and He shall be my Son."

The Bride of the Lamb

ONE OF THE ANGELS SAID, "Come I will show you the bride of the Lamb." There, on a high mountain, stood the new Jerusalem in all its radiance and glory, with new walls, new gates with the names of the twelve tribes of Israel, and the names of the twelve apostles of the Lamb.

The city is four square and fifteen hundred miles around. The walls and gates are adorned with every kind of jewel and metal, and the streets are paved with gold.

The Temple Is the Lord

THERE IS NO TEMPLE, AS the Lord God Almighty and the Lamb are the temple. There is no sun or moon, for the glory of the Lord is its light, and the lamp is the Lamb. Nothing unclean can enter the city, only those whose names are written in the Lamb's Book of Life.

Through the city flows the river of life, bright as crystal, flowing from the throne of God and the Lamb. There, on either side, is the Tree of Life, with twelve kinds of fruit, bearing its fruit once a month. The leaves of the tree are for healing of the nations.

Behold the Lamb (Jesus) Is Coming Soon!

"BEHOLD, I AM COMING SOON, and my reward is with Me, to render to every man according to what he has done. I am the Alpha and the Omega, the beginning and the end. Blessed are those who wash their robe, for they have the right to the Tree of Life and can enter by the gates of the city.

"Outside of the gates are the sorcerers, immoral persons, the murderers, the idolaters, and those who practice lying. If anyone adds to this book, God shall add to him the plagues that are written in the book. Yes, I come quickly!"

What Is the Meaning of the Book of Revelation?

THE BOOK OF REVELATION, WRITTEN around AD 95 and believed to have been written by the apostle John, shows Christ as one who was and who is to come again.

Marvel not nor be discouraged by the inability to understand totally all the happenings in the book of Revelation or the sequence of it, for only Almighty God knows its true meaning and eventful timing. But do understand its intention of God's final and apocalyptic end-time judgment on the evil people of the earth.

Jesus Christ is the King of Kings and Lord of Lords, and the book of Revelation shows (1) the things of the past, (2) the things of the present, and (3) the things of the future ... for the Lord God lives in the past, present and future all at one time.

The book characterizes what will happen to the wicked and evil ones on earth when Almighty God releases the seven seals, the seven trumpets, and the seven bowls of wrath.

Jesus Christ, the Alpha and the Omega, called the Word of God, comes this time as a warrior filled with righteous indignation. His eyes are like a flame of fire, and out of His mouth shoots a sharp swift sword to smite the nations.

It foretells of the gathering of the kings of the earth for the final battle of Armageddon, where the Lord consumes the enemies of Israel with fire and brimstone.

Afterward, the Lord God binds Satan, the beast, and the false prophet and tosses them into the bottomless pit of fire and sulfur forever. Then a new heaven, earth, and Jerusalem, the bride of Christ, will appear ready for all who are found worthy.

Jesus will then sit at the right hand of Father God and open the Book of Life to judge the living and the dead. The living will live in the eternal peace, joy, and love with the Lord. The dead, who cursed God and His Son, will be cast outside the gates of heaven into the bottomless pit, where they will wail and weep and gnash their teeth in great anguish and despair, and the evilness in them will still curse God.

The book of Revelation is a final call for all to accept Jesus as their Lord and Savior. Now is the time to repent and ask for Almighty God's forgiveness, to amend your life with the help of Christ's grace (unmerited favor), and to accept Jesus as your Lord and Savior. In doing so you, too, are written into the Lamb's Book of Eternal Life.

A Saving End-Time Prayer

Father God, I ask for your forgiveness of my past sins, for I have so offended you. And I accept the sacrificial blood of your only begotten Son, Jesus Christ, as payment and redemption of my sins.

Father, I accept Jesus as my Lord and Savior. O Lord, I also ask for Jesus' Holy Spirit to enter my mind, body, heart, soul, and spirit so that I may be raised up at the end times and found worthy to have my name written into the end-time Lamb's Book of Life.

Dear Jesus, I ask for your intercessory prayers and grace to guide me in amending my ways. O Lord, please make me a vessel with the guidance of Your Spirit of Wisdom to know right from wrong and to help others in obtaining their name in the Lamb's Book of Eternal Life.

And I thank you so much, Lord Jesus, for your multitude of tender and intercessory mercies in hearing my prayer.

A perfect place to find the peace and joy of the Lord God is to visit the Bible Walk, located at 500 Tingley Avenue, Mansfield, Ohio 44905. Close to one million visitors who visited there have come away healed—physically, spiritually, mentally, emotionally, socially, psychologically, or financially. The Bible Walk is an indoor, lifelike setting with various biblical scenes. Shown here is a visualization of one of the scenes.

To visit individually or with a group, call 419-524-0139 or toll free #800-222-0139.

John 3:16 For God so loved the world that He gave His only begotten Son, Jesus Christ, that whosoever believes in Him should not perish, but have everlasting life.

Signs of the End Times

MATHEW 24:37 So IT WAS at the time of Noah, so it will be at the coming of the Son of Man.

Wars, rumors of wars,
disobedient children, lawlessness,
increase in third-world starvation, rampant disease,
universal upheaval of stars, ocean,
volcanoes, tsunamis, hurricanes, tornadoes,
plagues, divorces, unchecked fornication,
homosexuality, adultery,
excessive greed, arrogant pride,
loss of jobs and income, worldwide demonic activity,
constant danger and fear, total despair and hopelessness,
heightened anxiety, distrust everywhere,
economic turmoil, false friendships, whirlwind of
    worldwide travel,
disproportionate number of restaurants,
upheaval in world currency, complete electrical blackouts
    in the world,
world stock market plummets, increase in rape,
    kidnapping,
and ransoms, overload in hospitals, psychological
    breakdowns,
hives, shingles, and rashes from nerves,

rash of heart attacks, stomach problems, and cancers
   from stress,
suicides everywhere, break-ins of
banks and other financial institutions, robberies
   constantly,
civil decency eradicated,
little if any religious fervor, no belief in God,
and unrighteous, sinful ways fill the earth.

False Prophets

Matthew 24:3–14 The disciples asked the Lord, "What shall
be the signs of the coming and the end of the world?" Jesus
answered, "Many false prophets shall come saying, 'I am the
Christ' and shall deceive many; there will be wars and rumors
of wars, and nation shall rise up against nation; there shall be
famine, pestilence and earthquakes, then they shall deliver you
to be afflicted and put to death for my name's sake; betrayal will
run high and iniquity will abound, and the love for God will
wax cold; the gospel of the Lord shall be preached throughout
the world and then the end shall come—and you, that endure
until the end, shall be saved."

Here's What the Angels Who Obey God Do for You

First, you should know the various types of angels. There are:

The Archangels—Michael, Gabriel, Raphael, Uriel, Sealtiel, Jhudiel, and Barochiel
(*Note:* Various faiths have different names for some of the archangels.)
1st Sphere of Angels—seraphim, cherubim, and thrones
2nd Sphere of Angels—dominions, virtues, and powers
3rd Sphere of Angels—principalities, angels, and guardian angels

The above angels completely obey the Lord God and serve the needs of His people on earth. First and foremost, they serve Almighty God, and in doing so, they obediently serve the needs of the human race.

There are angels for the stars, the moon, the planets, the rivers, the seas, the oceans, the winds, music, history, math, or any subject available to man. There is a special angel to stand guard over you, if you let him.

The Lord tells you to call unto Him with your gains or losses, for He will send an emissary of angels to watch and care for your needs.

Just listen to the beautiful music or enlightened inventions that entertain and ensure that God's people do not perish, and you will soon see where each and all that is created was inspired by one of God's appointed angels.

When you pray, the Lord knows your needs even before you utter them. And your request may not be what you want, but it will be what is best for you at that particular time, delivered by angelic beings sent specifically to solve your dilemma.

It is not that the angels merely *serve* us, it is more that we *need* them. It matters not what you are trying to complete, just ask God to intervene, and you will *see the substance of things hoped for; the evidence of things not seen* take place.

And your request will always be fulfilled in the "eleventh hour." That way, you know for certain it was the divine intervention of the Lord's commissioned angels. It is wise to remember always that the Lord God is sovereign, and He shares not His glory with anyone or thing. And His answer always comes at the eleventh hour.

These are the angels who obey and serve God and mankind, not the ones who demonically work to oppress and enslave mankind to sinful, unrighteous ways. And it is the good angels that send the bad angels scurrying away when you call on Almighty God for help in any situation, for there are no catch-22s when the Lord intervenes.

Psalm 91:11 For God has commanded His angels to be about you, and they guard you in all your ways.

The Gifts of the Holy Spirit and Spirit of Wisdom

THE SPIRIT OF WISDOM PROVIDES a person with *knowledge* (facts) about the Lord, Jesus Christ. The facts are arranged in such an order that the person then gains *understanding* of God's precepts and commandments. Next, the person gains *wisdom* to decipher what is right and what is wrong or what is true and what is false pertaining to given facts. And finally, the person gains *vision*, which is the power to see ahead or have foresight to see how the given facts can be used in future beneficial ways so that mankind does not perish.

The Spirit of Wisdom is a tree of life to those who strive to possess her. She gives riches and honor, yea, durable riches and honor. She is more precious than rubies or fine gold. She puts a crown of honor upon the heads of those who exult her. And she will test all your ways.

The Holy Spirit brings unspeakable joy and miraculous healing to those who call on him. The Holy Spirit heals people physically, spiritually, socially, psychologically, and financially. It is the Holy Spirit that works to bring honor and glory unto

Father God and His only begotten Son, Jesus Christ. When a person is filled with the Holy Spirit, he or she lays hands on others and fills them with joy and healing power.

It is the accompaniment of the Almighty God's Holy Spirit and Spirit of Wisdom that allows one to have knowledge, understanding, wisdom, and vision, along with the power to bring joy and healing unto others. The inculcation of the Holy Spirit and the Spirit of Wisdom comes only when a person's thoughts, words, and deeds are pure gold in the eye of the Lord God.

And it was the inculcation of God's Holy Spirit that raised Jesus from the dead, and it is the same Holy Spirit—if you repentantly ask for it—that will raise you during the end times. Remember that the Holy Spirit is referred to as "He," and the Spirit of Wisdom is referred to as "She."

Both are gifts from Almighty God unto those who accept Jesus Christ as their Lord and Savior. There is no better time than now to repent of all your sinful ways and ask the Lord God for both the Holy Spirit and the Spirit of Wisdom to enter your mind, heart, soul, and spirit. Amen.

Romans 1:11 For I long to see you, that I may impart unto you some spiritual gift to the end that you may be established righteously.

The Baptism of Water, Fire, and Discernment

WHEN ONE IS COMPLETELY BAPTIZED, the person's total body is submerged underwater. This shows that the baptized person has surrendered his entire mind, body, heart, soul, and spirit to the Lord Jesus Christ. Knowing that Jesus was baptized in water by John the Baptist, how much more should you be baptized, also.

Early warriors used to go down under but keep one arm above the water with a sword in their hand, waving it so as to say, "I still have the right to fight off my enemies." Such warlike people forget that it is the Lord who stands with them in battle, more than their own personal being. For the Lord says, "It is not by horse and chariot, or by spear or sword that you are saved, but by my very spirit and intervening angels."

Baptism of fire is when the Holy Spirit enters one's mind, heart, soul, and spirit and the person becomes "born again." The person's body then becomes a temple of the living spirit of Christ Jesus. And again, this Holy Spirit is the very being that will raise you at the end times. Once imbued with the Holy Spirit, the born-again believer becomes on "fire" to spread this newly found spiritual knowledge and understanding to others.

A person receives discernment when he is imbued with the Spirit of Wisdom. The Spirit of Wisdom, like the Holy Spirit, is a gift from God to those whose thoughts, words, and deeds are tested by going through the hot burning furnace of life's complexities and who, overcoming them, become like pure, fine gold. Only then will the Lord God award the crown of "Wisdom."

Acts 2:38 Then Peter said unto them, "Repent and be baptized every one of you in the name of Jesus Christ for the remission of sins, and you shall receive the gift of the Holy Spirit."

Here Are the Four Trials the Newly "Born-Again" Christian Will Undergo from the Serpent Satan

First, Satan will let the birds of the air pick clean as many of the "seeds" (words of God) planted in the mind, heart, soul, and spirit of the newly born-again believer. This is where Satan steals and makes the Word of God seem counterfeit and of no intrinsic value to the newly born-again believer. He does this by false accusations about the Bible and the life and miracles of Christ.

Second, Satan will have some of the seeds fall on the pathway, and the sun will unmercifully bake them. This is Satan bringing the affliction of trials and tribulations of anguish, persecution, oppression, and distressing woe upon the newly born-again believer, hoping to discourage him or her from accepting Jesus as his Savior.

Third, Satan will have some of the seeds fall into the thorns and bushes and make the newly born-again believer lose his way to the path of salvation. This is Satan bringing the cares and riches of the world to the believer, hoping to cause him to seek plenteous wealth rather than the abundance of God's blessings.

241

Fourth, Satan completely loses out in trying to win over the newly born-again believer, as some of the seeds fall on the good soil and are deeply planted in the mind of the believer, who then spreads the seeds of Christ to others, ten and a hundredfold. Satan's serpent bag of tricks—that is, placing doubt and slanderous belittling, bringing affliction and oppression, and dangling untold wealth—are totally rejected by the true born-again believer. And the believer, spiritually on fire, spreads the word of Christ like a vast flame. Upon being born again, will you successfully run Satan's deceiving gauntlet? Will you spread God's word, or will you backslide into Satan's serpent den of iniquity?

Matthew 16:23 Then Jesus turned and said unto Peter, "Get you behind me, Satan, for you are an offence unto me; for you savor not the things that be of God, but those that be of men."

The Deadly Sins

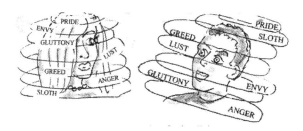

IT IS IRONIC THAT THE final end-time battle nervously teeters on three basic religions: Judaism, Islam, and Christianity.

In the world today, there are roughly 2.2 billion Christians. According to the Vatican, Islam has now overtaken the Christian population. And there are reportedly fifteen million Jews. Rounding out other religions, there are around nine hundred million Hindus, one billion Buddhist Chinese, as well as other smaller religions, not excluding the various cults and atheistic groups.

Wars have always been fought as people, and nations are more concerned about "getting" rather than "giving." Mankind's selfish "me-first" attitude comes about as Satan makes us forget that we are all brothers and sisters of the same ancestral, genetic dust. Once we acknowledge that helping each other is the key to survival, the peace and joy of the Lord springs forth across the world.

This is best illustrated by the fable of a man who dies and enters hell. There, he sees people starving. Although the people have huge bowls of soup in front of them, the ladle they are using is so long that after dipping it into the soup, they cannot get the nourishment into their mouth. This disturbed him as he was whisked away unto heaven.

And there in heaven, to his continued discouragement, he sees the people with the same big bowl of soup in front of them and with that long-handled spoon. Suddenly, his disheartened sadness turned to bubbling joy, as he watches the people feed each other rather than just trying to feed themselves.

Throughout the centuries, various prophets have prophesied how the precepts of the Lord annihilate the seven deadly sins:

humbleness subdues pride   sharing removes covetousness
chastity negates lust   patience quells anger
temperance diets gluttony   love nullifies envy
cleanliness washes away sloth

Shown above is how virtue wins over vice. Fear is the starter button for vice. . Remember, when fear knocks on your door and you answer it in faith, there is never anyone or anything there!

Hebrews 11:1 Jesus' faith is the substance of things hoped for—the substance of things not seen.

How Satan Activates the Seven Deadly Sins

To ACTIVATE THE SEVEN DEADLY sins, Satan places the element of alarm or impending apprehension in the mind of a person, people, or nation to set off the sinful elements of pride, covetousness, lust, anger, gluttony, envy, and sloth.

Did you not see that Joseph's brothers were fearfully zealous of his being over them, so their pride, envy, anger, and covetousness cast him into a well? And how the lust of Potiphar's wife had Joseph cast into prison. The interpretation of a butler's dream by Joseph determined that the gluttony of the baker would have the king impale his head upon a stake. In all the above instances, the sloth of not keeping God's word clean and fresh in their mind brought about destructive circumstance.

So, when fear knocks on your door, always answer it in faith, and you will never find anyone or anything there! For, as Hebrews 11:1 tells you, "Faith is the substance of things hoped for, the evidence of things not seen."

And always remember to value God's people.

One time, the Lord had me stop in traffic, turn around, and tell a hobo that the Lord loves him. The hobo, who was shouting obscenities to those passing by, was mouthy, dirty, and smelled. I walked up to him very reluctantly and said,

"The Lord sent me here to tell you He loves you." Whereas, he was calling people various uncouth names, he looked up at me and replied, "I'm not saying a word to you, baldy." While I was not bald, but sort of thin at the front of my head, I smiled and thought, *Lord, you really are testing me, aren't you?* God wants to make sure we do not feel we are better than others. This is an early step to negate any root of pride.

You see, if you just know the name of the president of a company and not the name of the janitor, you are passing judgment. At least try to get the janitor's name, even if you do not remember it. It is a beginning of not judging people, and learning to value all of them.

And when a person secretly tells you something, do not betray his or her trust. It is to be locked in your own mind and not relayed to others. So, you value not only the person, you also value what he or she tells you.

When you begin to value others, they begin to value you. And in doing so, the Lord God will even make your enemies considerate unto you.

Matthew 7:1–3 Judge not, that you be not judged. For how you judge, you shall be judged, and with what measure you mete, it shall be measured unto you. So why behold the spec in your brother's eye, when you consider not the beam in your own eye.

Repent!

WHEN YOU COME RIGHT DOWN to it, we have all committed at least one of the violations listed in this book. And we might have breached all of them in one way or another in our thoughts or words. It is well worth remembering that the Lord said, "If we think anything evil, we have, in spirit, already done it!"

It is a worthy task to stand guard over our deeds as well as our thoughts and words, as the Lord God knows what lies deep in our heart.

And when you come face to face with Him, all your good and bad thoughts, words, and deeds will jump out of you to be weighed, measured, and accounted for in the Lamb's Book of Life.

Look over the transgressions listed in this book, as well as others you have committed in your life. Reflect on them, and ask for the Lord's mercy and grace to wash clean your mind, heart, soul, and spirit.

Time is truly drawing nigh for many of us, without our even knowing it, even before the Lord Jesus' return. Our life is like a blade of grass, ready to be stepped upon by unforeseen things in life.

Get yourself rapture ready by confessing your sins to the Lord, asking Him to blot out your transgression with His multitude of tender mercies, repenting those sins completely, and asking Jesus' Holy Spirit to enter the temple of your body.

From there, find a good, spirit-filled church and fellowship with other true believers; financially support your church; aid others in need; and read the Bible throughout (over and over). With the help of the Holy Spirit, you will understand it. Carefully spread the Word of God to others who may need it; rid yourself of all foul language and lewdness; and change your reading material, pictures on the wall, movies, and other habits not conducive to your mind and spirit.

Then, you will find the joy, peace, love, and sublime salvation of the Lord.

Proverbs: 28:13 He that covers his sins shall not prosper; but he who confesses and forsakes them shall have mercy.

From the Palace (Heaven) to the Pit (Hell)

From the Palace (Heaven) to the Pit (Hell)

SHOWN ABOVE IS THE LADDER leading to the palace (heaven) or the pit (hell). The four work virtue rungs of the ladder are (1) industry, (2) ingenuity, (3) integrity, and (4) perseverance.

The application of all four of these above work virtues leads one to the palace here on earth and to the afterlife in heaven. The lack of any one of the work virtues starts a downward spiral to the pit, or hell bound.

There is a scripture for each work virtue.

For industry, the scriptures say, "Watch the ant, thy sluggard; consider her ways and be wise."

For ingenuity, the scriptures say, "I wisdom give knowledge to witty inventions, so my people do not perish."

For integrity, the scriptures say, "If you cannot be trusted with the small, you cannot be trusted with the large."

For perseverance, the scripture say, "Run the good race until it is finished."

The word "industry" refers to a person who has diligence, vigilance, pursuit, zeal, is hardworking, businesslike, intent, wide-awake, spirited, and enterprising in his or her everyday work habits.

The word "ingenuity" refers to a person who has inventive talent, perception, skill, resourcefulness, sharpness, aptitude, discernment, proficiency, readiness, dexterity, and an adept flair for what they are pursuing.

The word "integrity" refers to a person who has soundness of moral principles, character, goodness, virtue, honor, trustworthiness, fidelity, loyalty, justness, and a pure righteousness in his or her work ethics.

The word "perseverance" refers to a person who has steadfastness, tenacity, patience, stamina, determination, resoluteness, doggedness, courage, firmness, strength of purpose, and toughness of mind to complete a given objective or goal.

Now, a person might say to you, "I know a person who has the industry, ingenuity, and perseverance, but they have very little if any integrity and appear to be successful. What do you have to say about that?"

The answer is simple and easy. If you see a person utilizing three of the work virtues and is successful, without incorporating integrity in his or her work, you can be sure that person might continue to be successful here on earth, but in doing so, loses his or her soul for all eternity and is bound for the pit of fire and sulfur unless he or she repents.

So, do not negate integrity in your work. Many who do not use integrity (if they be of the Lord) get caught almost immediately. The Lord God will chastise and punish you, as He instantly corrects those who believe in Him.

Be careful of people without integrity. Even if they have the other three work virtues, the person without integrity most generally will either destroy you, your organization, or his or her own career.

Once again, if you neglect any of the four work virtues, your chance of success is very limited. This week, look at the newspapers, magazines, computer, and TV to see the many people who have fallen into the pit from something that was missing in their work virtues.

When I was driving to work one day, I asked the Lord, "Why is integrity so important?"

I was shown a hundred-story building and one that was only two stories high. Then I was told, "If I used the same material in the hundred-story building that I used in the two-story building, the hundred-story building would collapse because of the lack of the quality (the integrity) of the material used. The same thing relates to people. If they lack integrity, they will eventually collapse from their lofty height somewhere along the line."

That very night I went home and read in the paper where a top officer in the government lost his lofty position because of the lack of integrity.

Remember the four work virtues. Write them in your heart. Oh, there are times when you will fall short of one or more of them, for the Lord will never compromise truth (integrity), but we are never to give up trying. Repent and turn things around the right way and continue on.

If you incorporate the four work virtues in your efforts, you will become successful. If you don't, you will never get higher than the two-story building.

2 Peter 1:5–7 And besides giving all diligence in your efforts, be sure to add your faith virtue. And to that add knowledge, self-control, patience, and brotherly kindness.

The Good and Bad Angels

EVERYONE HAS A GUARDIAN ANGEL. Some do not believe that, but it is nevertheless true. The Lord God protects us with His angels. As you know, there are archangels, powers, principalities, thrones, dominions, virtues, seraphim, and cherubim, angels and guardian angels with specific jobs to do.

Now, you know that Satan copies all that the Lord God creates. So, Satan applies his demon (fallen angel) to each person, especially to those he feels are working feverishly for the Lord's people. And Satan will overload demons on people and places that are considered holy—like pastors, priests, rabbis, holy shrines, and other venerable places of worship.

You can notice and become fully aware when the fallen angel is competing with your guardian angel. Whenever you want to do something that is slightly wrong, whatever it may be, you sense a little light going out as you start to enter into a shadowy darkness. At that moment, you will not want anyone to know what you are thinking, saying, or doing that is unrighteous in its nature.

As quick as your think, say, or do something wrong, you will notice that you first and foremost will not want anyone to see you hiding in that darkness of thought, word, or deed. So, always stay in the "light" of your thoughts, words, and deeds, and you will benefit immensely in spiritual and physical rewards.

Now, a person might say the good angel is on your right

shoulder and the bad angel is on your left shoulder. However, they both hover around you. And it is your choice—as God gives you a free will—to decide if you want to live your life in the darkness of Satan or in the light of the Lord God.

As the old saying goes, "You cannot stop a bird from flying over your head, but you can prevent it from building a nest in your hair."

As soon as your thoughts or eyes turn toward the dark side, know it, change it, and say a short prayer, like, "Lord, guide my eyes and my thoughts. For You are the 'Light' of my life."

Psalm 91:11 For He shall give His angels charge over you in all your ways.

The Blessing or Curse Conclusion

"Behold, I the Lord God set before you this day a blessing or a curse. A blessing if you obey the commandments of the Lord God, and a curse if you not obey the commandments of the Lord God." (Deuteronomy 11:26–28)

The Blessing (Book of Deuteronomy) The Curse

The Blessing (Book of Deuteronomy)	The Curse
I will drive out all enemy nations before you.	I will bring a nation against you from a far end of the earth.
You will possess greater nations than yourself.	I will set up a heathen enemy against you.
Every where you place your foot will be yours.	I will utterly perish you off your own land.
No man will be able to stand up against you.	I will scatter you amongst the heathen nations.
Your days will be multiplied.	Death and disease will shorten your life.
I will multiply the fruits of your womb and the fruits of your fields and trees.	The locust and storms will consume your land and trees.
I will take away all your sickness and plagues.	Sickness, plagues and disease will ravage your land and people.

You shall walk and live the very Word of God.	I will give you over to the evil powers and principalities that roam the earth.
I shall provide you with the wisdom to solve all problems.	You will be void of my wisdom and sink in confusing despair.
I will make you prosper in all that you desire.	Your attempts to obtain your goals will be thwarted.

Deuteronomy 12:1 These are the statutes and ordinances you are to observe, that the Lord God has given to you, all the days that you live upon the earth.

Be Careful How You Judge

Which brings up the poem of the man who
Heavenly bound;
wanted to know who else was around.

Upon sheepishly entering the Pearly Gate
there to his roving, wondering eye
stood many of people in hopeful wait.

Stepping inside the angelic portal walls, he
breathed in deeply and wanted to shout,
"I made it" letting it all out.

Amidst the clouds of wonder
with beauty galore,
he again wondered, "Who else is
here besides me?" once more.

Glancing over the crowd inside,
"My goodness," he miffed and
upset he cried.

There standing in spiritual guise
stood his snooty neighbor,
the neighborhood gossiper,
the spiteful, the double dealing,

the liars and others to his
distasteful surprise.

"Lord, O Lord how can this be,"
with his hands upheld in earnest plea.

"Hush," said the Lord standing above
all there, "for these same people
you judge are all wondering
how you got here."

On the next pages, you will learn how they all arrived in heaven.

Answer: From all their sins they humbly relented,
and Heaven sent when they truly repented.

Reflective Afterthought

WRITING THIS BOOK IS SOMETHING that emotionally, spiritually, and mentally tossed me around: left, right, up, and down. For in no way am I someone who can tell others what is right or what is wrong. All I tried to do is write what I felt I was led to convey.

Hopefully, many of you will embrace this book, as it may have taken you on a more spiritual awareness journey. And, I am just as sure, some of you will look for the first window out of which you will pitch this book, either physically or mentally.

In no way can anyone read this book and accept each and every detail. Books are made to accept, reject, or modify.

It is worth noting again that the Lord God never compromises truth, but we are to never give up trying. In essence, this means that no matter how much you try, you will somehow always fall short of the Ten Commandments and the many moral factors listed in this book.

Then, what is the point?

The point is that we will always need Jesus Christ to intervene on our behalf to Father God for our shortcomings in our unrighteous thoughts, words, or deeds.

You see, if we were perfect—which we are not—we would not need Jesus. We would become filled with pride and self-righteousness.

But, I can assure you that you should refrain from making the same sinful mistake time and time again Even the demons believe in God and tremble in fear, yet over and over again, they commit the same evil.

If you are going through a rough time right now, the Lord may be bringing this upon you in order to restore you in His name. Whenever times are tough, immediately begin praising God out loud. There is no catch-22 with the Lord. He restores all things in their proper place. He is sovereign. He rules all. He has the answer to all and everything in the universe

And He looks for that courageous obedience of faith in His people. Believe it. Mentally lock into it. And He will bring you through anything and everything.

1 Peter 5:6–7 Humble yourself before God that He may exult you in due time. Cast all your cares upon Him, and He will take care of you.

Simeon and Anna

(Luke 2:24–40)

As the scriptures state, "A thousand years of man is only one day to the Lord God."

It has been four thousand years—with the passing of Adam and Eve; Abraham; Moses; the Judges; David; Solomon; the various prophets, such as, Isaiah, Jeremiah, and Daniel; and the Roman evasion. And another two thousand years since the prophet Simeon and the prophetess Anna came on board in Jerusalem to prophesy the coming of the Messiah, Jesus.

The Holy Ghost revealed to Simeon and Anna that they would not see death until they saw the Messiah. Both Simeon and Anna fasted and prayed continuously for years in the temple.

(Here, it is worth noting that the Book of Life (in which all are written who are to enter the kingdom of God) and the Book of Death (in which all who are written are cast into the Lake of Fire) are opened during the ten-day period of Rosh Hashanah (the Jewish New Year) and Yom Kippur (the Jewish Day of Atonement). So again, it is important to know the Jewish roots of Christianity. They are closely and inextricably tied together.)

Finally, both Joseph and Mary brought the baby Jesus (after He was circumcised) to the temple to present Him to the Lord God. There in the temple, the sacrifice of a pair of turtledoves or two young pigeons was to be offered unto the Lord.

When Simeon saw the baby Jesus, he held Him in his arms, blessed God, and said, "My eyes have seen salvation."

Anna also came in the room of the temple and when seeing baby Jesus, said, "All who look upon Him in Jerusalem will see redemption."

It is important that we all become like Simeon and Anna as we wait in high expectation of Jesus' return, for yes indeed, Jesus is coming soon.

And as we wait, continue in your daily duties, for during the end times not only your will your faith will be judged but also your works.

Revelation 22:12 Behold, I come quickly, and my reward is with me to give to each person according to their works.

Acknowledgments

King James Bible
New American Bible

And to my lovely wife, Gail, who always
sacrifices for me and the family. And to my
beloved family members who have played an
instrumental part in our life due to the love,
nurturing, and care of my wife.
It is imperative to know that neither myself
nor any of my family members are not without
fault; like everyone else, we spiritually dust
ourselves off in Christ's mercy and grace and
continue on in life's journey to heaven.

In conclusion, I again, want to thank and
praise Father God, my Savior, Jesus Christ,
the Holy Spirit and the Spirit of Wisdom.
And for the intercessory prayers of the angels,
apostles, martyrs, prophets, and saints to the
Lord God, on my behalf, to compete this book.

And a special thanks to Bill Warren, Wayne and Lisa
Dollard, Mike and Renee Russell, Peggy Bowers, Rand
Hofman, Joe Bruesch, and my spiritual mentors: Pastor Dick
Diamond, Reverend Jude Mili, and Pastor Keith Eggert.